THE

OLYNTHIACS

OF

DEMOSTHENES.

With Notes

FOR SCHOOLS AND COLLEGES.

By W. S. TYLER,

WILLISTON PROFESSOR OF GREEK IN AMHERST COLLEGE.

WIPF & STOCK · Eugene, Oregon

Wipf and Stock Publishers
199 W 8th Ave, Suite 3
Eugene, OR 97401

The Olyanthics of Demosthenes
With Notes
By Tyler, W. S.
ISBN 13: 978-1-60899-375-8
Publication date 1/21/2010
Previously published by Allyn and Bacon, 1893

PREFACE.

THIS edition of the Olynthiacs of Demosthenes is intended, as announced in the title-page, for schools and colleges, and is meant especially for the use of students in these institutions. In an age when, relatively and more emphatically than ever before, "life is short and art is long," and when, next to mathematics, perhaps, Greek is usually one of the first studies to be retrenched, other things being equal, that commentary will be the best on a Greek classic which gives the most *needed* guidance and assistance, and takes the least time in giving it. In such an age brevity and conciseness are demanded, and may well be regarded as prime qualities in helps to classical study. Notes on the Olynthiacs of Demosthenes ought especially to have something of the compactness of the Orations themselves. I have therefore aimed to help the student only where he needs help, to dispense with all superfluous and all *useless* comment which includes all notes that are *certain not to be used*, and to condense the entire book within the smallest possible compass. At the same time I have endeavored to point to the sources — grammars, lexicons, dictionaries, histories, and editions — from which, if he has the time and the inclination, the student may derive further knowledge or illustration, thus choosing to be a finger-board to guide his studies rather than a pack-horse or pony to carry him over the road, and deeming it far better that he should be taught and led to do the work wisely and well himself than to have it done for him.   With this view I have referred him or left him to go to the dictionary, which every student should have continually by him and should form the habit of consulting, for the geography of places and even for the knowledge of antiquities, except when it was essential to the understanding of the passage, or perchance the point was involved in some special difficulty or uncertainty. If any should question the necessity of so copious an introduction, or its consistency with the brevity which has been studied in the notes, I have only to say, that regarding a pretty familiar acquaintance with the occasion and the circumstances as the first requisite to the interpretation or the appreciation of any work, I hoped that all this introductory matter would conduce directly to the understanding of the orations and to a fuller sympathy with the orator and the actors.

The text of this edition follows mainly that of Bekker's stereotype edition.   I have not hesitated, however, to depart from it, whenever there seemed to be sufficient reasons, which have usually been stated in the notes.   The editions and commentaries which I have most frequently consulted are those of J. H. Reiske, corrected and enlarged by G. H. Schäfer, London, 1823 ; W. Dindorf, Oxford, 1849, itself a *library* of notes and comments on Demosthenes ; K. H. Frötscher and K. H. Funkhänel, Leipsic, 1834 ; J. H. Vömel, Halle, 1856 ; A. Westermann, Leipsic, 1851 ; F. Franke, Leipsic, 1871 ; C. Rehdantz, Leipsic, 1873 ; R. Whiston, London, 1859 ; and G. H. Heslop, Oxford, 1872. I have usually compared them all in reference to difficult and disputed passages.   I have found the notes of Whiston,

Franke, and Rehdantz particularly sensible and suggestive. When I have thought the renderings in any of these editions particularly just and happy, I have often quoted them and given credit accordingly; and I am indebted to them for suggestion and confirmation in other instances in which I can only make this general acknowledgment. In my own renderings I have tried to follow the rule which I inculcate in my classes of giving as close and exact a translation as can be given in good idiomatic English, aiming *as far as possible* to make Demosthenes speak an English as compact, clear, pointed, and energetic as his own Greek, and believing, as I do with all my heart, that there can be no better discipline for the faculties of reason and speech in the schools than that which may be acquired by a faithful representation, a genuine *reproduction*, in our vernacular, if only that might be hoped for, of the Orations of Demosthenes.

W. S. TYLER.

AMHERST COLLEGE, April 20, 1875.

INTRODUCTION.

THE genius and eloquence of Demosthenes have perpetuated the memory of persons of whom we might otherwise have never heard, and invested with interest places of which we should otherwise have known little and for which we should have cared less. Philip and Olynthus, immortalized in his orations, have not only become familiar names in ancient history, but have given new words to the languages of modern Europe. The city to which the Olynthiacs of Demosthenes have given so much celebrity, claimed an antiquity scarcely less venerable than that of Athens herself. Its foundation was ascribed by some to a mythic son of Hercules, by others to a son of Strymon, the Thracian king. Lying near the head of the Toronaic gulf between the peninsulas of Pallene and Sithonia, surrounded by a fertile plain and favorably situated for navigation and commerce, it early became an important place and was at one time the head of a confederacy of over thirty cities in and near the great Chalcidic peninsula. Inhabited by the Bottiæi, it first makes its appearance in history as furnishing a contingent of troops to the army of Xerxes in the Persian war. Suspected, however, after the battle of Salamis, it was besieged and taken by Artabazus, and its inhabitants massacred, thus foreshadowing in the early history of Greece that more fatal overthrow which shortly preceded the subversion of Grecian liberty. Repeopled by Chalcidic Greeks, who had settled in the neighborhood from Chalcis, a colony of Athens in Eubœa, Olynthus now came more directly into the circle of Grecian states and entered upon a new career of diversified and eventful history. We cannot follow it in detail. Concisely it is as follows : Originally by descent and by natural affinity allied to Athens, but in the Peloponnesian War taking sides with Sparta, and thus securing an acknowledged independence ; usually on friendly terms with the earlier kings of Macedon, but gradually growing rich and powerful at their expense, now by inducing Pella, their chief city, to join the Olynthiac confederacy, and now through the voluntary cession of Lower Macedonia on the Thermaic Gulf by King Amyntas to save it from the Illyrians ; attracting most of the Chalcidic cities to its alliance by the liberality of its international principles and political spirit, but by this very prosperity awakening the envy and jealousy of Acanthus and Apollonia, and provoking them to join with Macedon in calling for the armed intervention of Sparta ; successfully resisting for a time the Lacedæmonians at the height of their power in a four years' war and inflicting upon them a terrible defeat in which they lost their general, but compelled by famine to sue for peace and submit to their hegemony ; on the decline of that hegemony, reuniting all the Chalcidians under its own supremacy, and even wresting Amphipolis from the Athenians, but in turn stripped by them of Methone, Potidæa, Toronea, and several other towns in the vicinity ; courted, flattered, and sought as an ally, both by Athens and by Philip, and vibrating now towards the one and now towards the other of these great powers, but attacked violently at length by all the forces of the latter and imperfectly succored and sustained by the former — Olynthus was finally betrayed into the hands of Philip, the city was destroyed, and the inhabitants, men, women, and children, were sold into slavery. The fall of Olynthus completed the conquest of the thirty-two Chalcidic cities, whose destruction was so complete that Demosthenes says in his third Philippic, five years afterwards, that their sites could hardly be found, and it might be supposed that they had never been inhabited.

A fuller history of the period after the accession of Philip to the throne may shed light on the relations of the Olynthians, Athenians, and Macedonians at the time of the Olynthian War, and may help the reader to a better understanding of the Olynthiac orations. Whiston has given it concisely and with careful reference to authorities: " This event (the accession of Philip) soon changed the position of affairs. The Athenians at first supported a rival, Argæus, in his claims to the throne, with a view of recovering Amphipolis (Diod., XVI. 3), and a portion of their forces, principally mercenaries, actually marched from Methone on the coast for thirty miles inland, where, with Argæus himself, they were attacked by Philip and obliged to surrender (c. Aristoc., § 144). But it was not Philip's policy to make enemies, so he allowed them to depart, and sent an embassy to Athens, with proposals of peace and friendship, professing also to give up all claims of his own to Amphipolis (Diod,. XVI. 3, 4 ; Grote, XI. 301), which, according to Diodorus, had already been evacuated by the Macedonian troops posted there by Philip's predecessor, Perdiccas (Grote, X. 516), to protect it against the Athenians (B. C. 359 – 58). Nevertheless, from whatever cause (Grote, XI. 306), the Athenians did not themselves make any attempt to occupy it : and Philip, as soon as he could, resolved to take advantage of their remissness by attacking it himself, while he deluded them with the assurance that he intended to restore it to them after capturing it (c. Aristoc., 138 ; De Halon., 28). But this promise he did not fulfil, and the Olynthians, alarmed at the conquest and the rapid extension of his power, thereupon sent to Athens to negotiate an alliance (Olynth., II. 20), but without success, for the Athenians still trusted the continued assurances of Philip. Repulsed in that quarter, they readily accepted the alliance which that politic monarch offered them, and received from him the cession of Potidæa, taken from the Athenians (B. C. 357) by their combined forces (Phil., II. 22 ; Grote, XI. 335). And even before this he had ceded to them the district and city of Anthemus, so that he effectually secured their friendship to himself and their hostility against Athens, while, without any formal declaration of war, he was commencing that series of aggressions which led to what was called the war of Amphipolis, and continued between the Athenians and himself for twelve years, till the peace of B. C. 346 (Fal. Leg. *passim*). But Philip and the Olynthians were too near neighbors to continue friends, their independence and progress being manifestly inconsistent with his ambitious aggrandizement. As his power and conquests extended, their conviction of this fact appears to have become more decided, for we read (c. Aristoc., 129) that in B. C. 352 – 51, probably after Philip's victories in Thessaly, they had again become the friends, though not as yet allies, of Athens. This change in their sentiments Philip appears to have considered, and perhaps with satisfaction, a sufficient reason for hostilities. Accordingly soon afterwards (Phil., I. 20) his troops invaded their territory, and in B. C. 350 – 49 (Grote, XI. 449), after recovering from an illness in Thrace, he commenced serious operations against

them by marching into Chalcidice. The *immediate cause*
of this attack is stated by Justin (VIII. 3) to have been
their reception and protection of his two half-brothers, a
brother of whom he had already put to death, and who
themselves escaped, for a time, the same fate by flight.
But this doubtless was only a pretext, not the real cause of
his hostility, nor do we even know when it was first put
forward. This attack was preceded by his previous reduc-
tion of several other Chalcidian towns, till the progress of
his conquests and their proximity to themselves at last induced the Olynthians to send to Athens with proposals for
an alliance, and to solicit its active co-operation against him.
This proposition was favorably received, as the Olynthians
would naturally expect ; for not long before the Athenians
themselves had expressed a wish that Olynthus might be
induced to act against Philip (Olyn., I. 7). The assembly
which was called to consider it was almost unanimous in
voting that assistance should be sent, though Demades
(Suidas s. v.) opposed it. But the conclusion of an alliance was a very different thing with the Athenians from
active co-operation with their allies, and therefore it was
that Demosthenes delivered his three Olynthiac orations
one after the other, pressing upon his reluctant fellow-
citizens the duty of vigorous action as well as wise deter-
mination. After his second speech, as it would seem, two
thousand *mercenaries* were despatched under the command
of Chares (Dionys., Epis. I. ad Amm. IX.) and some successes were achieved by him. The news created much
exultation at Athens, and the people began to fancy, not
only that they had rescued Olynthus, but that there was a
fair prospect of their punishing and humbling Philip (τοὺς
λόγους περὶ τοῦ τιμωρήσασθαι Φίλιππον ὁρῶ γιγνομένους). To
combat this delusion, to exhort his fellow-countrymen to
1*

still greater and personal exertions, — possibly, too, in consequence of a second embassy from Olynthus, — Demosthenes delivered his third Olynthiac. One specific measure which he then recommended was an expedition of Athenian citizens instead of foreign mercenaries. This plan, however, was not then adopted, nor do we know for certain whether the oration (delivered towards the end of B. C. 350) was productive of any immediate and practical results, for soon afterwards the Athenian forces were engaged in Euboea in putting down a revolt, probably instigated by Philip himself (De Pace, 5). From Euboea, in the first half of B. C. 349, a cavalry force of Athenian citizens crossed over to Olynthus, and Philochorus, an author quoted by Dionysius of Halicarnassus (Epis. I. ad Amm. IX.), states that Chares was despatched with a body of two thousand hoplites and three hundred horsemen, all citizens. This force, however, of Athenian citizens, as Mr. Grote suggests (XI. 467), was not sent till the latter part of the war, which continued two years and a half. We are further assured by Demosthenes (Fal. Leg., 301) that from first to last the Athenians despatched no less than ten thousand mercenaries and four thousand native troops and fifty triremes to assist their allies. But all to no purpose; their troops were badly commanded, and no really efficient aid was given till it was too late; and Olynthus finally fell by treachery into Philip's hands (B. C. 347)."

Such is the narrative which Whiston, following the lead of Grote, gives of the efforts of the Athenians to aid Olynthus, and such all that can be *known* with *certainty* of the effect of the Olynthiacs of Demosthenes on these transactions. The more common account, adopted by Becker in his "Demosthenes as Statesman and Orator," Thirlwall in his "History of Greece," etc., and generally accepted previous

to the appearance of Grote's History, ascribes to the Olynthiac orations a more direct and controlling influence in the
Olynthian War. In brief it is as follows : the three Olynthiac orations were occasioned by three successive embassies
from Olynthus asking military aid against the encroachments of Philip, and were followed by three successive
expeditions sent out from Athens for that purpose. The
first embassy, opposed by Demades, Eubulus, and others,
was warmly supported by Demosthenes, and a force of two
thousand mercenaries, under Chares, was sent for their
relief. But after skirmishing about the coast of Pallene
and capturing a few scattering bands of Macedonians, they
returned in triumph to Athens. Beaten in two engagements and driven within their walls, the Olynthians now
sent a second embassy. Demosthenes, in a second oration,
exerted all his energies to rouse the Athenians to exertions
worthy of the interests at stake and their former glory ;
and the people sent a force of four thousand mercenaries
and one hundred and fifty horse under Charidemus. The
Olynthians sallied forth to meet them, and were repulsed ;
and then the mercenaries resolved themselves into a band
of freebooters and plundered the territory which they were
sent to protect. A third embassy now entreated for an
army of citizens ; and Demosthenes seconded their request
in a third oration of still greater urgency and eloquence.
They accordingly voted an army of two thousand infantry
and three hundred cavalry consisting of citizen soldiers,
and summoned all Greece to resist the encroachments of
the common enemy.

Grote does not deny the sending of the three expeditions
mentioned by Dionysius on the authority of Philochorus,
but he finds insuperable objections against associating them
with the three orations of Demosthenes and supposing

them, as Dionysius does, to constitute the whole Olynthian War. "The Olynthian War," he says, "began in 350 B. C., and the three Olynthiacs of Demosthenes refer, in my judgment, to the first months of the war. But it lasted until the early spring of 347 B. C., so that the armaments mentioned by Philochorus may have occurred during the last half of the war. I cannot but think that Dionysius, being satisfied with finding *three* expeditions to Olynthus which might be attached as results to the *three* orations of Demosthenes, has too hastily copied out the three from Philochorus, and has assigned the date of 349 – 48 B. C. to the three *orations*, simply because he found that date given to the three *expeditions* by Philochorus " (Grote, XI. p. 467). The principal reason for separating the three expeditions from the three orations is found in the history of the Athenian expedition to Euboea. At the time when the third Olynthiac was delivered, no expedition of Athenian *citizens* had been sent to the aid of Olynthus. But Athenian citizens *were* sent thither, as above stated, from Euboea during the first half of 349 B. C. The inference is that the orations were all delivered prior to that sending. The simple fact that the Olynthiacs make no allusion to the Euboean expedition certainly favors the opinion that the orations preceded that agitating and important expedition (Grote, XI. p. 469). The question cannot be settled, although that question carries with it another, namely, the date of the Olynthiacs, which Grote, followed by Whiston, assigns to 350 B. C., but which is more commonly assigned to 349 – 48 B. C.

There is another vexed question which is more insoluble than these, and that relates to the order in which the three orations were delivered. In all the manuscripts as well as principal editions they are arranged in the order in which they are now numbered. But Dionysius cites them by

their first words in such a manner as to indicate that he reckoned the first as last, and the second and third as first and
second. And Grote accedes to the arrangement of Dionysius
so far as to place the second first, but he regards the first as
belonging in the second place, and holds the third as still
entitled to the place which it has always occupied. The
presumption is certainly in favor of the order which they
occupy in the manuscripts; and the preponderance of authority is in favor of the same arrangement, which had the
unanimous sanction of the ancient scholiasts, grammarians,
and rhetoricians, and also meets the approval of the majority of modern scholars. Petrenz, in his dissertations (1833
and 1834), has thoroughly canvassed the internal evidence,
and presented in a clear and strong light the arguments in
favor of the traditional order. Dindorf considers the argument conclusive, and has prefixed a summary of it to his
notes on the Olynthiacs. Westermann has reached the
same conclusion in the first part of his *Quæstiones Demos-
thenicæ* where he has devoted an elaborate treatise of eighty-
four pages to this question. Schaefer, Böhnecke, Vömel,
Rehdantz, and Kennedy also defend the order in which
they are edited. Thirlwall advocates the Dionysian order.
Grote, followed by Whiston, as we have seen, and by Müller,
in his " History of Greek Literature," agrees with Dionysius
in placing the second first, but adheres to the common
opinion in retaining the third as the last. This last point
may be regarded as substantially settled by the almost unanimous verdict of competent judges. Thirlwall now stands
almost alone in opposition to the spontaneous conviction or
feeling that the third oration alone was worthy to be and
must in fact have been the last oration of Demosthenes on
the subject of Olynthus. The order of the other two still
remains and is likely always to remain *sub judice*. The

order of the manuscripts cannot be allowed to *settle* the question of the chronological order, for on that principle the first Philippic which follows them in the manuscripts would precede them, since, by common consent, it was delivered prior to them. The argument from the contents of the two orations is so plausible on both sides that the advocate of either seems to have carried his point, till " his neighbor cometh and searcheth him," and is so far from conclusive that the very same acknowledged characteristic, as, for example, the particular and specially *Olynthiac* character of the first oration as compared with the confessedly general and *Philippic* cast of the second, has been adduced as an argument on both sides. Fortunately the value and interest of the orations do not depend on a knowledge of their chronological order ; hence some of the best recent editions, as, for instance, those of Franke, Rehdantz, and Heslop, either ignore the question or barely allude to it. Readers who are interested in it will do well to consult Grote's Appendix to Chap. LXXXVIII. Vol. XI. ; Thirlwall's Appendix to Vol. II. p. 501, Amer. ed. ; Whiston's Excursus, Vol. I. p. 68 ; and above all the dissertations of Petrenz, in Dindorf's Prolegomena to the Olynthiac Orations, Vol. I. pp. 8 – 22, and Westermann's treatise De Or. Ol. Demos. Ordine.

The Olynthiacs were called Philippics by Dionysius of Halicarnassus, who reckoned as such twelve orations all bearing more or less directly against Philip and all delivered in the course of about as many years (B. C. 352 – 340), and who numbered the Olynthiacs as the second, third, and fourth in the series.

Lasthenes and Euthycrates, of whom the former led the cavalry in the last battle before Olynthus and betrayed them into the hands of Philip, have been immortalized as

traitors by Demosthenes (De Cherson., 40 ; De Cor., 48).
The strong language of the orator in the former of these
passages has been understood to imply that they were put
to death. But the latter passage explains his meaning (see
note on De Cor., 48). The real state of the case is more
truly indicated by one of Plutarch's anecdotes which represents them as complaining that some of Philip's courtiers
had called them traitors. "The Macedonians," he is said
to have replied, "are blunt, rough folks : they call a spade
a spade." Nothing worse appears to have befallen them
than the disappointment of their ambitious aims, in the
utter ruin of the city where they had probably hoped to rule,
and the condition of exiles with the consciousness that they
were abhorred by the friends of their country and despised
by its enemies. (See Thirlwall, Vol. II. p. 209.)

ANALYSIS OF THE OLYNTHIACS.

One characteristic of these orations which cannot but
strike the modern reader is their brevity. The text in this
edition, as the reader will see, occupies only about ten pages
for each, and only a little over thirty pages in all. Mr.
Kennedy's translation of the orations fills a little over
twenty pages in Bohn's edition, giving an average of less
than seven pages to each. A modern orator would have
occupied five or ten times the space, without after all saying so much as our orator has said that was directly to the
point, and adapted simply to accomplish his object. Di-
rectness, simplicity, plainness, and clearness are also equally
characteristic of these orations. They are masterpieces of
art, and yet it is the art which conceals art. They are
highly artistic, but at the farthest possible remove from all
that is artificial. These qualities will be fully appreciated

only after a repeated reading of the orations. But the following analysis may serve to illustrate them and may also aid the reader's perception and remembrance of the plan and principal contents.

FIRST OLYNTHIAC.

The exordium, comprised in a single section, we might say in a single sentence, simply presents in a clear and striking light the reason why the people should give the orator, in common with other speakers, an attentive hearing. The second paragraph, consisting of the next eleven sections (2 – 12), states with equal clearness and conciseness the orator's advice to send immediate succor to Olynthus and his reasons for it, in which he skilfully mingles encouragement drawn from the spontaneous offer of so important and so natural an ally with warnings from the perpetual encroachments of the crafty and despotic Philip, and reproofs for their own negligence of the past and present, and fond but false hopes for the future. The next two sections (14, 15) exhibit forcibly in the light of the past the bankruptcy and ruin which must inevitably result from a continuance in the same course. The next three sections (16 – 18) develop in a manner worthy of the chief statesman as well as the first orator of Athens his definite plan for the relief of Olynthus, which is twofold: first, to send troops to protect the Chalcidic cities; and, second, to despatch another armament, partly naval and partly military, to ravage the territory of Philip. The next two sections (19, 20) relate to ways and means, and show how the Athenians can have money enough by a temporary appropriation of the theoric fund if they will; if they will not, by an extraordinary war-tax. Sections 21 – 24 are intended to encourage and stimulate

the people by an examination of the critical and uncertain
state of Philip's affairs, owing especially to the fickleness
and jealousy of the Thessalians and the free and indepen-
dent spirit of the Pæonians and Illyrians. In the next
three sections (25 – 27) the orator assures the Athenians
that they must take their choice, and now it is in their
power to choose, between meeting Philip at Olynthus and
fighting him at their own gates, and that in the latter case
the damage to the agricultural population alone in a single
campaign would exceed the whole expense of their late ten
years' war for the possession of Amphipolis. The conclusion — a single section and sentence like the exordium —
summons all classes, rich and poor, soldiers and orators, to
rally for the common weal which was no less the private
interest of them all, and ends with a brief prayer — only
five words — for a prosperous issue.

SECOND OLYNTHIAC.

The second Olynthiac is, as we have already intimated,
less distinctively Olynthiac and more Philippic than the first.
From this fact Grote draws an argument in favor of his
hypothesis, that the second oration was delivered first, for
the general purpose of rousing the indignation and hostility
of the Athenians against Philip, before the question of suc-
coring Olynthus had come before them with any urgency.
But the Greek Argument or Hypothesis prefixed to the
Greek text of the second Olynthiac explains this *Philippic*
cast of the oration by their fear and dread of Philip, which
it is now the orator's chief object to remove. "The Athenians had given a favorable reception to the Olynthian embassy and resolved to send them aid. And while they are
procrastinating and dreading an encounter with so formida-

B

ble an enemy as Philip, Demosthenes comes forward and endeavors to encourage them by showing how weak Philip really is : for he is an object of suspicion and distrust to his allies, and the Macedonians in themselves are anything but a great power." Such is the occasion of the oration as given in the ΥΠΟΘΕΣΙΣ and accepted by Petrenz, Westermann, and other advocates of the received order of the Olynthiacs. The first two sections constitute the exordium. The orator begins with the topic which was especially adapted to encourage the δεισιδαιμονέστεροι Ἀθηναῖοι, namely, the good-will of the gods manifested to them in all their history, but conspicuously manifest in the raising up at this crisis of an ally so near, of such considerable resources, and so irreconcilable to Philip; and he exhorts them not to be so base as, with their towns and fortresses, to give up also the allies and opportunities furnished them by the blessing of heaven. The next two sections (3, 4) contain the *statement* of his object, which is not to set forth the power and success of Philip, and thus rouse them to do their duty, but to show his true character, his essential weakness in himself, and the only source of his accidental strength, which was not in himself but in Athens. The next paragraph (§§ 5 – 8) convicts Philip of faithlessness and perjury by repeated instances in his dealings with the Olynthians and Thessalians as well as the Athenians, and predicts that he will fall by the very means by which he has risen; that the very men who have lifted him up when they thought he would further their own interests, would pull him down now that he was proved to be doing everything for himself. The two following sections (9, 10) insist on the necessary instability of all mere material resources, towns, fortresses, harbors, and the like, and the utter impossibility of building an enduring empire on the foundation of injustice, falsehood, and perjury. This is followed by a brief statement (11 – 13) of his advice, which is to send immediate succor to the Olynthians, to inform the Thessalians of this purpose and invite their co-operation, and, above all, to stop talking, in which their superiority was already too conspicuous, and begin to pay war-taxes, serve in the armies, and do their whole duty. The orator then proceeds (14 – 21) to expose analytically and at length the inherent weakness of Philip and his empire : he and his subjects have diametrically opposite interests ; *their* peace and prosperity are irreconcilable with the military glory which is *his* passion ; his troops have a reputation far beyond their deserts ; he is jealous and envious of his best officers and dismisses them ; and the rest, his favorites, are intemperate, licentious, drunkards and brigands, like himself ; his foreign wars have only weakened his resources, and a war on his frontiers will expose the rottenness of his power, as sickness brings out all the infirmities, wounds, and fractures of the natural body. True (22 – 29) Philip has been a fortunate man, and fortune is everything in human affairs. But he owes his success to his ceaseless toil and sleepless vigilance. Be as watchful and energetic as he is, nay, act as vigorously for your own rights and interests as you have often acted for those of the other Grecian states, and you are far more likely to enjoy the smiles of fortune and the blessing of heaven than Philip. Do your own duty in person ; see with your own eyes that your generals do theirs ; let your " classes " (συμμορίαι) pay war-taxes as they did in the good old times, and not, as they do now, manage politics, with an orator to preside on either side, a general under him, the three hundred to shout applause, and the rest of you attaching yourselves now to this party and now to that. In conclusion, then (30, 31), you must have done with all this ; you must equalize the privileges and the duties of all classes of the citizens ; you must all in rotation serve in the armies ; you must listen to the advice of all your orators, and choose the best measures, not those recommended by some popular favorite. Then you will not merely applaud the speaker at the moment, but yourselves afterwards when you see the improved state of your affairs.

THIRD OLYNTHIAC.

The third Olynthiac is just as clearly intended to moderate the excessive confidence of the people as the second was to inspire them with courage in undue despondency. Doubtless, as the Argument of Libanius affirms, the Athenians had sent succors to Olynthus, and their mercenaries had gained some partial and temporary success, which set the popular heart and tongue all on fire with zeal for the punishment of Philip. This furnishes the key to the introduction (1, 3), in which the orator naïvely informs them that their advisers had simply mistaken the *question*, which was not how to punish Philip, but how to save themselves ; in other words, they were guilty of the absurdity which logicians call ὕστερον πρότερον in talking about the end before they had made sure of the beginning. He then in a single section (3) states his difficulty, which is not what the people ought to do in the present critical emergency, but how he could persuade them to do it. As preliminary to such persuasion he reminds them (4, 5) of the magnificence of their votes three or four years previous, when Philip was reported to be attacking a fortress in Thrace, and the long delay and farcical disparity in its execution, and the abandonment even of that abortive effort in consequence of a report that Philip was sick or dead ; and then

(6 – 9) he **exhorts** them not to lose the opportunity now afforded by the war of Olynthus against Philip, which they had taken so much pains to foment, and warns them of the disgrace and danger that must result from such neglect. And now coming to the question of ways and means, he advances boldly (10 – 13) to the recommendation or demand which, unpopular and even odious as it is to the Athenian populace, is the orator's main counsel and reliance, namely, that they should annul the existing laws in regard to the theoric fund, which cut the very sinews of war, partly by distributing to those who stayed at home the money which should support the army abroad, and partly by shielding from deserved punishment those who shirk the service. Then he returns (14 – 20) to the necessity of carrying their resolves into execution, reminds them of the obvious fact that resolutions never execute themselves; that action, though posterior in order of time to speaking and voting, is prior and superior in efficiency; and now there is an imperative necessity, not for mutual censure and recrimination, not for vows, prayers, and good wishes, and not even for wise counsels, so much as for immediate vigorous action. It is no new thing for Athenian citizens to serve in the armies and sacrifice their private interest and pleasure to the public good (21 – 29); this was just what their ancestors did when they won such victories and reared such monuments; when they ruled over willing Greece, and at the same time deposited millions in the Athenian treasury; when they reared public edifices which were the admiration and envy of the world, while the private residences of Aristides, Miltiades, and the other leading men were no more imposing than those of their neighbors. How unlike to all this were the manners and the measures of the present rulers, and how different the results! The radical cause of the difference (30 – 32) is,

that the people and their rulers have changed places ; that whereas the people were formerly the masters and the rulers their servants, now, on the other hand, the rulers are the masters, and the people, their humble servants, are delighted if they distribute among them the theoric fund and exhibit the Boëdromia for their entertainment.   The only way to honor and save their country (33 – 36) is to act worthy of themselves and their ancestors ; to break away from this degrading and demoralizing servitude ; to give up this life of shows and this living on a miserable pittance of show-money, or rather to receive the money, and, serving in person in the army, to subsist themselves and carry on the war by that means, and thus, without taking away the rights or adding to the duties of Athenian citizens, only equalizing the burdens and systematizing the service, to stand at the post bequeathed to them by their ancestors, and do for themselves what they so highly honor in others.   The oration ends, where it begins, with the gods, in a brief and simple prayer that they may choose such measures as will conduce to the prosperity of the state and the well-being of all the people.

How Bulwer could ever have persuaded himself — to say nothing of his readers — that such orations as these were suited to amuse and captivate the theatre-going Athenians, but not to convince and persuade a modern audience, is beyond my comprehension.   They are wonderfully plain, simple, direct, straightforward, business-like, and statesman-like.   There is not a word in them for the mere purpose of tickling the ear, affording amusement, or creating a sensation.   There is not a figure or an illustration merely for the sake of ornament.   They are the perfection of good common sense, plain matter of fact, forcible thought, and conclusive reasoning, or rather unquestionable *reason*, animated by suitable feeling and expressed in a style of absolute fitness and transparent clearness ; and such orations, while they were especially adapted to move and win those to whom they were immediately addressed, are at the same time suited to convince and persuade intelligent hearers and readers in every age. The sufficient proof of this is found in the fact that cultivated readers in all ages, in spite of changing and adverse circumstances, *have* given them a verdict of unanimous approval.

ΔΗΜΟΣΘΕΝΟΥΣ

ΟΛΥΝΘΙΑΚΟΣ Α.

Ἀντὶ πολλῶν ἄν, ὦ ἄνδρες Ἀθηναῖοι, χρημάτων ὑμᾶς ἑλέσθαι νομίζω, εἰ φανερὸν γένοιτο τὸ μέλλον συνοίσειν τῇ πόλει περὶ ὧν νυνὶ σκοπεῖτε. ὅτε τοίνυν τοῦθ᾽ οὕτως ἔχει, προσήκει προθύμως ἐθέλειν ἀκούειν τῶν βουλομένων συμβουλεύειν· οὐ γὰρ μό- 5 νον εἴ τι χρήσιμον ἐσκεμμένος ἥκει τις, τοῦτ᾽ ἂν ἀκούσαντες λάβοιτε, ἀλλὰ καὶ τῆς ὑμετέρας τύχης ὑπολαμβάνω πολλὰ τῶν δεόντων ἐκ τοῦ παραχρῆμα ἐνίοις ἂν ἐπελθεῖν εἰπεῖν, ὥστ᾽ ἐξ ἁπάντων ῥᾳδίαν τὴν τοῦ συμφέροντος ὑμῖν αἵρεσιν γενέσθαι. 10

Ὁ μὲν οὖν παρὼν καιρός, ὦ ἄνδρες Ἀθηναῖοι, 2 μόνον οὐχὶ λέγει φωνὴν ἀφιεὶς ὅτι τῶν πραγμάτων ὑμῖν ἐκείνων αὐτοῖς ἀντιληπτέον ἐστίν, εἴπερ ὑπὲρ σωτηρίας αὐτῶν φροντίζετε· ἡμεῖς δ᾽ οὐκ οἶδ᾽ ὅντινά μοι δοκοῦμεν ἔχειν τρόπον πρὸς αὐτά. ἔστι δὴ τὰ 15 γ᾽ ἐμοὶ δοκοῦντα ψηφίσασθαι μὲν τὴν βοήθειαν, καὶ παρασκευάσασθαι τὴν ταχίστην ὅπως ἐνθένδε βοη- θήσετε καὶ μὴ πάθητε ταὐτὸν ὅπερ καὶ πρότερον, πρεσβείαν δὲ πέμπειν ἥτις ταῦτ᾽ ἐρεῖ καὶ παρέσται

1   Α

3 τοῖς πράγμασιν· ὡς ἔστι μάλιστα τοῦτο δέος, μὴ
πανοῦργος ὢν καὶ δεινὸς ἄνθρωπος πράγμασι χρῆσθαι, τὰ μὲν εἴκων, ἡνίκα ἂν τύχῃ, τὰ δ᾽ ἀπειλῶν
(ἀξιόπιστος δ᾽ ἂν εἰκότως φαίνοιτο), τὰ δ᾽ ἡμᾶς
5 διαβάλλων καὶ τὴν ἀπουσίαν τὴν ἡμετέραν, τρέψηται καὶ παρασπάσηταί τι τῶν ὅλων πραγμάτων.
4 οὐ μὴν ἀλλ᾽ ἐπιεικῶς, ὦ ἄνδρες Ἀθηναῖοι, τοῦθ᾽, ὃ
δυσμαχώτατόν ἐστι τῶν Φιλίππου πραγμάτων, καὶ
βέλτιστον ὑμῖν· τὸ γὰρ εἶναι πάντων ἐκεῖνον ἕνα
10 ὄντα κύριον καὶ ῥητῶν καὶ ἀπορρήτων, καὶ ἅμα
στρατηγὸν καὶ δεσπότην καὶ ταμίαν, καὶ πανταχοῦ
αὐτὸν παρεῖναι τῷ στρατεύματι, πρὸς μὲν τὸ τὰ τοῦ
πολέμου ταχὺ καὶ κατὰ καιρὸν πράττεσθαι πολλῷ
προέχει, πρὸς δὲ τὰς καταλλαγάς, ἃς ἂν ἐκεῖνος
15 ποιήσαιτο ἄσμενος πρὸς Ὀλυνθίους, ἐναντίως ἔχει.
5 δῆλον γάρ ἐστι τοῖς Ὀλυνθίοις ὅτι νῦν οὐ περὶ
δόξης οὐδ᾽ ὑπὲρ μέρους χώρας πολεμοῦσιν, ἀλλ᾽
ἀναστάσεως καὶ ἀνδραποδισμοῦ τῆς πατρίδος, καὶ
ἴσασιν ἅ τ᾽ Ἀμφιπολιτῶν ἐποίησε τοὺς παραδόντας
20 αὐτῷ τὴν πόλιν καὶ Πυδναίων τοὺς ὑποδεξαμένους·
καὶ ὅλως ἄπιστον, οἶμαι, ταῖς πολιτείαις ἡ τυραννίς,
6 ἄλλως τε κἂν ὅμορον χώραν ἔχωσι. ταῦτ᾽ οὖν
ἐγνωκότας ὑμᾶς, ὦ ἄνδρες Ἀθηναῖοι, καὶ τἄλλ᾽ ἃ
προσήκει πάντα ἐνθυμουμένους φημὶ δεῖν ἐθελῆσαι
25 καὶ παροξυνθῆναι καὶ τῷ πολέμῳ προσέχειν, εἴπερ
ποτέ, καὶ νῦν, χρήματα εἰσφέροντας προθύμως καὶ
αὐτοὺς ἐξιόντας καὶ μηδὲν ἐλλείποντας. οὐδὲ γὰρ

λόγος οὐδὲ σκῆψις ἔθ' ὑμῖν τοῦ μὴ τὰ δέοντα ποιεῖν
ἐθέλειν ὑπολείπεται. νυνὶ γάρ, ὃ πάντες ἐθρυλεῖτε, 7
ὡς Ὀλυνθίους ἐκπολεμῶσαι δεῖ Φιλίππῳ, γέγονεν αὐτόματον, καὶ ταῦθ' ὡς ἂν ὑμῖν μάλιστα συμ-
φέροι. εἰ μὲν γὰρ ὑφ' ὑμῶν πεισθέντες ἀνείλοντο 5
τὸν πόλεμον, σφαλεροὶ σύμμαχοι καὶ μέχρι του
ταῦτ' ἂν ἐγνωκότες ἦσαν ἴσως· ἐπειδὴ δ' ἐκ τῶν
πρὸς αὐτοὺς ἐγκλημάτων μισοῦσι, βεβαίαν εἰκὸς
τὴν ἔχθραν αὐτοὺς ὑπὲρ ὧν φοβοῦνται καὶ πεπόν-
θασιν ἔχειν. οὐ δεῖ δὴ τοιοῦτον, ὦ ἄνδρες Ἀθηναῖοι, 8
παραπεπτωκότα καιρὸν ἀφεῖναι, οὐδὲ παθεῖν ταὐτὸν 11
ὅπερ ἤδη πολλάκις πρότερον πεπόνθατε. εἰ γάρ,
ὅθ' ἥκομεν Εὐβοεῦσι βεβοηθηκότες καὶ παρῆσαν
Ἀμφιπολιτῶν Ἱέραξ καὶ Στρατοκλῆς ἐπὶ τουτὶ τὸ
βῆμα, κελεύοντες ἡμᾶς πλεῖν καὶ παραλαμβάνειν 15
τὴν πόλιν, τὴν αὐτὴν παρειχόμεθ' ἡμεῖς ὑπὲρ ἡμῶν
αὐτῶν προθυμίαν ἥνπερ ὑπὲρ τῆς Εὐβοέων σωτηρίας, εἶχετ' ἂν Ἀμφίπολιν τότε καὶ πάντων τῶν
μετὰ ταῦτα ἂν ἦτε ἀπηλλαγμένοι πραγμάτων. καὶ 9
πάλιν ἡνίκα Πύδνα, Ποτίδαια, Μεθώνη, Παγασαί, 20
τἆλλα, ἵνα μὴ καθ' ἕκαστα λέγων διατρίβω, πο-
λιορκούμενα ἀπηγγέλλετο, εἰ τότε τούτων ἑνὶ τῷ
πρώτῳ προθύμως καὶ ὡς προσῆκεν ἐβοηθήσαμεν
αὐτοί, ῥᾴονι καὶ πολὺ ταπεινοτέρῳ νῦν ἂν ἐχρώμεθα
τῷ Φιλίππῳ. νῦν δὲ τὸ μὲν παρὸν ἀεὶ προϊέμενοι, 25
τὰ δὲ μέλλοντα αὐτόματ' οἰόμενοι σχήσειν καλῶς,
ηὐξήσαμεν, ὦ ἄνδρες Ἀθηναῖοι, Φίλιππον ἡμεῖς, καὶ

κατεστήσαμεν τηλικοῦτον ἡλίκος οὐδείς πω βασιλεὺς γέγονε Μακεδονίας. νυνὶ δὴ καιρὸς ἥκει τις
οὗτος ὁ τῶν Ὀλυνθίων αὐτόματος τῇ πόλει, ὃς οὐδε-
10 νός ἐστιν ἐλάττων τῶν προτέρων ἐκείνων. καὶ
5 ἔμοιγε δοκεῖ τις ἄν, ὦ ἄνδρες Ἀθηναῖοι, δίκαιος λο-
γιστὴς τῶν παρὰ τῶν θεῶν ἡμῖν ὑπηργμένων καταστάς, καίπερ οὐκ ἐχόντων ὡς δεῖ πολλῶν, ὅμως
μεγάλην ἂν ἔχειν αὐτοῖς χάριν, εἰκότως· τὸ μὲν γὰρ
πολλὰ ἀπολωλεκέναι κατὰ τὸν πόλεμον τῆς ἡμετέ-
10 ρας ἀμελείας ἄν τις θείη δικαίως, τὸ δὲ μήτε πάλαι
τοῦτο πεπονθέναι πεφηνέναι τέ τινα ἡμῖν συμμα-
χίαν τούτων ἀντίρροπον, ἂν βουλώμεθα χρῆσθαι,
τῆς παρ᾽ ἐκείνων εὐνοίας εὐεργέτημ᾽ ἂν ἔγωγε θείην.
11 ἀλλ᾽ οἶμαι, παρόμοιόν ἐστιν ὅπερ καὶ περὶ τῆς τῶν
15 χρημάτων κτήσεως· ἂν μὲν γάρ, ὅσα ἄν τις λάβῃ,
καὶ σώσῃ, μεγάλην ἔχει τῇ τύχῃ τὴν χάριν, ἂν δ
ἀναλώσας λάθῃ, συνανάλωσε καὶ τὸ μεμνῆσθαι τὴν
χάριν. καὶ περὶ τῶν πραγμάτων οὕτως οἱ μὴ χρη-
σάμενοι τοῖς καιροῖς ὀρθῶς, οὐδ᾽ εἰ συνέβη τι παρὰ
20 τῶν θεῶν χρηστόν, μνημονεύουσι· πρὸς γὰρ τὸ
τελευταῖον ἐκβὰν ἕκαστον τῶν πρὶν ὑπαρξάντων
κρίνεται. διὸ καὶ σφόδρα δεῖ τῶν λοιπῶν ἡμᾶς, ὦ
ἄνδρες Ἀθηναῖοι, φροντίσαι, ἵνα ταῦτ᾽ ἐπανορθωσάμενοι τὴν ἐπὶ τοῖς πεπραγμένοις ἀδοξίαν ἀποτριψώ-
12 μεθα. εἰ δὲ προησόμεθα, ὦ ἄνδρες Ἀθηναῖοι, καὶ
26 τούτους τοὺς ἀνθρώπους, εἶτ᾽ Ὄλυνθον ἐκεῖνος κατα-
στρέψεται, φρασάτω τις ἐμοὶ τί τὸ κωλῦον ἔτ᾽ αὐτὸν

ἔσται βαδίζειν ὅποι βούλεται. ἆρα λογίζεταί τις
ὑμῶν, ὦ ἄνδρες Ἀθηναῖοι, καὶ θεωρεῖ τὸν τρόπον
δι' ὃν μέγας γέγονεν ἀσθενὴς ὢν τὸ κατ' ἀρχὰς Φίλιππος; τὸ πρῶτον Ἀμφίπολιν λαβών, μετὰ ταῦτα
Πύδναν, πάλιν Ποτίδαιαν, Μεθώνην αὖθις, εἶτα 5
Θετταλίας ἐπέβη· μετὰ ταῦτα Φερὰς, Παγασὰς, 18
Μαγνησίαν, πάνθ' ὃν ἐβούλετο εὐτρεπίσας τρόπον
ᾤχετ' εἰς Θράκην· εἶτ' ἐκεῖ τοὺς μὲν ἐκβαλὼν τοὺς
δὲ καταστήσας τῶν βασιλέων ἠσθένησε· πάλιν
ῥαΐσας οὐκ ἐπὶ τὸ ῥᾳθυμεῖν ἀπέκλινεν, ἀλλ' εὐθὺς 10
Ὀλυνθίοις ἐπεχείρησεν· τὰς δ' ἐπ' Ἰλλυριοὺς καὶ
Παίονας αὐτοῦ καὶ πρὸς Ἀρύμβαν καὶ ὅποι τις ἂν
εἴποι παραλείπω στρατείας.

Τί οὖν τις ἂν εἴποι ταῦτα λέγεις ἡμῖν νῦν; ἵνα 14
γνῶτε, ὦ ἄνδρες Ἀθηναῖοι, καὶ αἴσθησθε ἀμφότερα, 15
καὶ τὸ προΐεσθαι καθ' ἕκαστον ἀεί τι τῶν πραγμάτων ὡς ἀλυσιτελές, καὶ τὴν φιλοπραγμοσύνην ᾗ
χρῆται καὶ συζῇ Φίλιππος, ὑφ' ἧς οὐκ ἔστιν ὅπως
ἀγαπήσας τοῖς πεπραγμένοις ἡσυχίαν σχήσει. εἰ
δ' ὁ μὲν ὡς ἀεί τι μεῖζον τῶν ὑπαρχόντων δεῖ 20
πράττειν ἐγνωκὼς ἔσται, ὑμεῖς δὲ ὡς οὐδενὸς ἀντιληπτέον ἐρρωμένως τῶν πραγμάτων, σκοπεῖσθε εἰς
τί ποτ' ἐλπὶς ταῦτα τελευτῆσαι. πρὸς θεῶν, τίς 15
οὕτως εὐήθης ἐστὶν ὑμῶν ὅστις ἀγνοεῖ τὸν ἐκεῖθεν πόλεμον δεῦρο ἥξοντα, ἂν ἀμελήσωμεν; ἀλλὰ 25
μὴν εἰ τοῦτο γενήσεται, δέδοικα, ὦ ἄνδρες Ἀθηναῖοι,
μὴ τὸν αὐτὸν τρόπον, ὥσπερ οἱ δανειζόμενοι ῥᾳδίως

ἐπὶ τοῖς μεγάλοις τόκοις μικρὸν εὐπορήσαντες χρόνον ὕστερον καὶ τῶν ἀρχαίων ἀπέστησαν, οὕτω
καὶ ἡμεῖς ἐπὶ πολλῷ φανῶμεν ἐρραθυμηκότες, καὶ
ἅπαντα πρὸς ἡδονὴν ζητοῦντες πολλὰ καὶ χαλεπὰ
5 ὧν οὐκ ἡβουλόμεθα ὕστερον εἰς ἀνάγκην ἔλθωμεν
ποιεῖν, καὶ κινδυνεύσωμεν περὶ τῶν ἐν αὐτῇ τῇ
χώρᾳ.

16   Τὸ μὲν οὖν ἐπιτιμᾶν ἴσως φήσαι τις ἂν ῥᾴδιον
καὶ παντὸς εἶναι, τὸ δ' ὑπὲρ τῶν παρόντων ὅ τι
10 δεῖ πράττειν ἀποφαίνεσθαι, τοῦτ' εἶναι συμβούλου.
ἐγὼ δὲ οὐκ ἀγνοῶ μέν, ὦ ἄνδρες Ἀθηναῖοι, τοῦθ',
ὅτι πολλάκις ὑμεῖς οὐ τοὺς αἰτίους ἀλλὰ τοὺς ὑστά-
τους περὶ τῶν πραγμάτων εἰπόντας ἐν ὀργῇ ποιεῖσθε, ἄν τι μὴ κατὰ γνώμην ἐκβῇ· οὐ μὴν οἴομαι
15 δεῖν τὴν ἰδίαν ἀσφάλειαν σκοποῦνθ' ὑποστείλασθαι
17 περὶ ὧν ὑμῖν συμφέρειν ἡγοῦμαι. φημὶ δὴ διχῇ
βοηθητέον εἶναι τοῖς πράγμασιν ὑμῖν, τῷ τε τὰς
πόλεις τοῖς Ὀλυνθίοις σῴζειν καὶ τοὺς τοῦτο ποιή-
σοντας στρατιώτας ἐκπέμπειν, καὶ τῷ τὴν ἐκείνου
20 χώραν κακῶς ποιεῖν καὶ τριήρεσι καὶ στρατιώταις
ἑτέροις· εἰ δὲ θατέρου τούτων ὀλιγωρήσετε, ὀκνῶ
18 μὴ μάταιος ὑμῖν ἡ στρατεία γένηται. εἴτε γὰρ
ὑμῶν τὴν ἐκείνου κακῶς ποιούντων ὑπομείνας τοῦτο
Ὄλυνθον παραστήσεται, ῥᾳδίως ἐπὶ τὴν οἰκείαν
25 ἐλθὼν ἀμυνεῖται· εἴτε βοηθησάντων μόνον ὑμῶν εἰς
Ὄλυνθον ἀκινδύνως ὁρῶν ἔχοντα τὰ οἴκοι προσκαθεδεῖται καὶ προσεδρεύσει τοῖς πράγμασι, περιέσται

τῷ χρόνῳ τῶν πολιορκουμένων. δεῖ δὴ πολλὴν καὶ διχῇ τὴν βοήθειαν εἶναι.

Καὶ περὶ μὲν τῆς βοηθείας ταῦτα γιγνώσκω· 19 περὶ δὲ χρημάτων πόρου, ἔστιν, ὦ ἄνδρες Ἀθηναῖοι, χρήματα ὑμῖν, ἔστιν ὅσα οὐδενὶ τῶν ἄλλων ἀνθρώ- 5 πων στρατιωτικά, ταῦτα δὲ ὑμεῖς οὕτως ὡς βούλεσθε λαμβάνετε. εἰ μὲν οὖν ταῦτα τοῖς στρατευομένοις ἀποδώσετε, οὐδενὸς ὑμῖν προσδεῖ πόρου, εἰ δὲ μή, προσδεῖ, μᾶλλον δ' ἅπαντος ἐνδεῖ τοῦ πόρου. τί οὖν ἄν τις εἴποι, σὺ γράφεις ταῦτ' εἶναι στρατιω- 10 τικά; μὰ Δί' οὐκ ἔγωγε. ἐγὼ μὲν γὰρ ἡγοῦμαι 20 στρατιώτας δεῖν κατασκευασθῆναι καὶ ταῦτ' εἶναι στρατιωτικὰ καὶ μίαν σύνταξιν εἶναι τὴν αὐτὴν τοῦ τε λαμβάνειν καὶ τοῦ ποιεῖν τὰ δέοντα, ὑμεῖς δὲ οὕτω πως ἄνευ πραγμάτων λαμβάνετε εἰς τὰς ἑορτάς. 15 ἔστι δὴ λοιπόν, οἶμαι, πάντας εἰσφέρειν, ἂν πολλῶν δέῃ, πολλά, ἂν ὀλίγων, ὀλίγα. δεῖ δὲ χρημάτων, καὶ ἄνευ τούτων οὐδὲν ἔστι γενέσθαι τῶν δεόντων. λέγουσι δὲ καὶ ἄλλους τινὰς ἄλλοι πόρους, ὧν ἕλεσθε ὅστις ὑμῖν συμφέρειν δοκεῖ, καὶ ἕως ἐστὶ καιρός, ἀν- 20 τιλάβεσθε τῶν πραγμάτων.

Ἄξιον δὲ ἐνθυμηθῆναι καὶ λογίσασθαι τὰ πράγ- 21 ματα, ἐν ᾧ καθέστηκε νυνί, τὰ Φιλίππου. οὔτε γάρ, ὡς δοκεῖ καὶ φήσειέ τις ἂν μὴ σκοπῶν ἀκριβῶς, εὐτρεπῶς, οὐδ' ὡς ἂν κάλλιστ' αὐτῷ τὰ παρόντ' ἔχει· 25 οὔτ' ἂν ἐξήνεγκε τὸν πόλεμόν ποτε τοῦτον ἐκεῖνος, εἰ πολεμεῖν ᾠήθη δεήσειν αὐτόν, ἀλλ' ὡς ἐπιὼν ἅπαντα

τότε ἤλπιζε τὰ πράγματα ἀναιρήσεσθαι, κᾆτα διέψευσται.   τοῦτο δὴ πρῶτον αὐτὸν ταράττει παρὰ
γνώμην γεγονός, καὶ πολλὴν ἀθυμίαν αὐτῷ παρέχει,
22 εἶτα τὰ τῶν Θετταλῶν.   ταῦτα γὰρ ἄπιστα μὲν ἦν
5 δήπου φύσει καὶ ἀεὶ πᾶσιν ἀνθρώποις, κομιδῇ δ',
ὥσπερ ἦν, καὶ ἔστι νῦν τούτῳ.   καὶ γὰρ Παγασὰς
ἀπαιτεῖν αὐτόν εἰσιν ἐψηφισμένοι, καὶ Μαγνησίαν
κεκωλύκασι τειχίζειν.   ἤκουον δ' ἔγωγε τινῶν ὡς
οὐδὲ τοὺς λιμένας καὶ τὰς ἀγορὰς ἔτι δώσοιεν αὐτῷ
10 καρποῦσθαι· τὰ γὰρ κοινὰ τὰ Θετταλῶν ἀπὸ τούτων δέοι διοικεῖν, οὐ Φίλιππον λαμβάνειν.   εἰ δὲ
τούτων ἀποστερηθήσεται τῶν χρημάτων, εἰς στενὸν
κομιδῇ τὰ τῆς τροφῆς τοῖς ξένοις αὐτῷ καταστήσε-
23 ται.   ἀλλὰ μὴν τόν γε Παίονα καὶ τὸν Ἰλλυριὸν
15 καὶ ἁπλῶς τούτους ἅπαντας ἡγεῖσθαι χρὴ αὐτονό-
μους ἥδιον ἂν καὶ ἐλευθέρους ἢ δούλους εἶναι· καὶ
γὰρ ἀήθεις τοῦ κατακούειν τινός εἰσι, καὶ ἄνθρωπος
ὑβριστής, ὥς φασιν.   καὶ μὰ Δί' οὐδὲν ἄπιστον
ἴσως· τὸ γὰρ εὖ πράττειν παρὰ τὴν ἀξίαν ἀφορμὴ
20 τοῦ κακῶς φρονεῖν τοῖς ἀνοήτοις γίγνεται, διόπερ
πολλάκις δοκεῖ τὸ φυλάξαι τἀγαθὰ τοῦ κτήσασθαι
24 χαλεπώτερον εἶναι.   δεῖ τοίνυν ὑμᾶς, ὦ ἄνδρες Ἀθηναῖοι, τὴν ἀκαιρίαν τὴν ἐκείνου καιρὸν ὑμέτερον νομί-
σαντας ἑτοίμως συνάρασθαι τὰ πράγματα, καὶ
25 πρεσβευομένους ἐφ' ἃ δεῖ καὶ στρατευομένους αὐτοὺς
καὶ παροξύνοντας τοὺς ἄλλους ἅπαντας, λογιζομέ-
νους, εἰ Φίλιππος λάβοι καθ' ἡμῶν τοιοῦτον καιρὸν

καὶ πόλεμος γένοιτο πρὸς τῇ χώρᾳ, πῶς ἂν αὐτὸν
οἴεσθε ἑτοίμως ἐφ᾽ ὑμᾶς ἐλθεῖν. εἶτ᾽ οὐκ αἰσχύ-
νεσθε, εἰ μηδ᾽ ἃ πάθοιτ᾽ ἄν, εἰ δύναιτ᾽ ἐκεῖνος,
ταῦτα ποιῆσαι καιρὸν ἔχοντες οὐ τολμήσετε;

Ἔτι τοίνυν, ὦ ἄνδρες Ἀθηναῖοι, μηδὲ τοῦθ᾽ ὑμᾶς 25
λανθανέτω, ὅτι νῦν αἵρεσις ἔστιν ὑμῖν πότερ᾽ ὑμᾶς 6
ἐκεῖ χρὴ πολεμεῖν ἢ παρ᾽ ὑμῖν ἐκεῖνον. ἐὰν μὲν
γὰρ ἀντέχῃ τὰ τῶν Ὀλυνθίων, ὑμεῖς ἐκεῖ πολεμή-
σετε καὶ τὴν ἐκείνου κακῶς ποιήσετε, τὴν ὑπάρχουσαν καὶ τὴν οἰκείαν ταύτην ἀδεῶς καρπούμενοι· ἂν 10
δ᾽ ἐκεῖνα Φίλιππος λάβῃ, τίς αὐτὸν ἔτι κωλύσει
δεῦρο βαδίζειν; Θηβαῖοι; μὴ λίαν πικρὸν εἰπεῖν 26
ᾖ, καὶ συνεισβαλοῦσιν ἑτοίμως. ἀλλὰ Φωκεῖς; οἱ
τὴν οἰκείαν οὐχ οἷοί τε ὄντες φυλάττειν, ἐὰν μὴ
βοηθήσηθ᾽ ὑμεῖς. ἢ ἄλλος τις; ἀλλ᾽ ὦ τᾶν οὐχὶ 15
βουλήσεται. τῶν ἀτοπωτάτων μέντ᾽ ἂν εἴη, εἰ ἃ
νῦν ἄνοιαν ὀφλισκάνων ὅμως ἐκλαλεῖ, ταῦτα δυνη-
θεὶς μὴ πράξει. ἀλλὰ μὴν ἡλίκα γ᾽ ἐστὶ τὰ διά- 27
φορα ἐνθάδε ἢ ἐκεῖ πολεμεῖν, οὐδὲ λόγου προσδεῖν
ἡγοῦμαι. εἰ γὰρ ὑμᾶς δεήσειεν αὐτοὺς τριάκοντα 20
ἡμέρας μόνας ἔξω γενέσθαι καὶ ὅσα ἀνάγκη στρα-
τοπέδῳ χρωμένους τῶν ἐκ τῆς χώρας λαμβάνειν,
μηδενὸς ὄντος ἐν αὐτῇ πολεμίου λέγω, πλέον ἂν
οἶμαι ζημιωθῆναι τοὺς γεωργοῦντας ὑμῶν ἢ ὅσα εἰς
ἅπαντα τὸν πρὸ τοῦ πόλεμον δεδαπάνησθε. εἰ δὲ δὴ 25
πόλεμός τις ἥξει, πόσα χρὴ νομίσαι ζημιώσεσθαι;
καὶ προσέσθ᾽ ἡ ὕβρις καὶ ἔτι ἡ τῶν πραγμάτων

1*

αἰσχύνη, οὐδεμιᾶς ἐλάττων ζημίας τοῖς γε σώ-
φροσιν.

28   Πάντα δὴ ταῦτα δεῖ συνιδόντας ἅπαντας βοηθεῖν
καὶ ἀπωθεῖν ἐκεῖσε τὸν πόλεμον, τοὺς μὲν εὐπόρους,
5 ἵν' ὑπὲρ τῶν πολλῶν ὧν καλῶς ποιοῦντες ἔχουσι
μικρὰ ἀναλίσκοντες τὰ λοιπὰ καρπῶνται ἀδεῶς, τοὺς
δ' ἐν ἡλικίᾳ, ἵνα τὴν τοῦ πολεμεῖν ἐμπειρίαν ἐν τῇ
Φιλίππου χώρᾳ κτησάμενοι φοβεροὶ φύλακες τῆς
οἰκείας ἀκεραίου γένωνται, τοὺς δὲ λέγοντας, ἵν' αἱ
10 τῶν πεπολιτευμένων αὐτοῖς εὔθυναι ῥᾴδιαι γένωνται,
ὡς ὁποῖ' ἄττ' ἂν ὑμᾶς περιστῇ τὰ πράγματα, τοιοῦ-
τοι κριταὶ καὶ τῶν πεπραγμένων αὐτοῖς ἔσεσθε.
χρηστὰ δ' εἴη παντὸς εἵνεκα.

ΟΛΥΝΘΙΑΚΟΣ Β.

Ἐπὶ πολλῶν μὲν ἄν τις ἰδεῖν, ὦ ἄνδρες Ἀθηναῖοι, 1
δοκεῖ μοι τὴν παρὰ τῶν θεῶν εὔνοιαν φανερὰν γιγνομένην τῇ πόλει, οὐχ ἥκιστα δὲ ἐν τοῖς παροῦσι
πράγμασι· τὸ γὰρ τοὺς πολεμήσοντας Φιλίππῳ
γεγενῆσθαι καὶ χώραν ὅμορον καὶ δύναμίν τινα κεκ- 5
τημένους, καὶ τὸ μέγιστον ἁπάντων, τὴν ὑπὲρ τοῦ
πολέμου γνώμην τοιαύτην ἔχοντας ὥστε τὰς πρὸς
ἐκεῖνον διαλλαγὰς πρῶτον μὲν ἀπίστους, εἶτα ἑαυτῶν
πατρίδος νομίζειν ἀνάστασιν, δαιμονίᾳ τινὶ καὶ θείᾳ
παντάπασιν ἔοικεν εὐεργεσίᾳ. δεῖ τοίνυν, ὦ ἄνδρες 2
Ἀθηναῖοι, τοῦτ᾽ ἤδη σκοπεῖν αὐτούς, ὅπως μὴ χεί- 11
ρους περὶ ἡμᾶς αὐτοὺς εἶναι δόξομεν τῶν ὑπαρχόντων, ὡς ἔστι τῶν αἰσχρῶν, μᾶλλον δὲ τῶν αἰσχί-
στων, μὴ μόνον πόλεων καὶ τόπων ὧν ἡμέν ποτε
κύριοι φαίνεσθαι προϊεμένους, ἀλλὰ καὶ τῶν ὑπὸ 15
τῆς τύχης παρασκευασθέντων συμμάχων καὶ καιρῶν.

Τὸ μὲν οὖν, ὦ ἄνδρες Ἀθηναῖοι, τὴν Φιλίππου 3
ῥώμην διεξιέναι καὶ διὰ τούτων τῶν λόγων προτρέ-
πειν τὰ δέοντα ποιεῖν ὑμᾶς οὐχὶ καλῶς ἔχειν ἡγοῦμαι. διὰ τί; ὅτι μοι δοκεῖ πάνθ᾽, ὅσ᾽ ἂν εἴποι τις 20
ὑπὲρ τούτων, ἐκείνῳ μὲν ἔχειν φιλοτιμίαν, ἡμῖν δ᾽
οὐχὶ καλῶς πεπρᾶχθαι. ὁ μὲν γὰρ ὅσῳ πλείονα

ὑπὲρ τὴν ἀξίαν πεποίηκε τὴν αὑτοῦ, τοσούτῳ θαυ-
μαστότερος παρὰ πᾶσι νομίζεται· ὑμεῖς δὲ ὅσῳ
χεῖρον ἢ προσῆκε κέχρησθε τοῖς πράγμασι, τοσούτῳ
4 πλείονα αἰσχύνην ὠφλήκατε. ταῦτα μὲν οὖν παρα-
5 λείψω. καὶ γὰρ εἰ μετ' ἀληθείας τις, ὦ ἄνδρες
Ἀθηναῖοι, σκοποῖτο, ἐνθένδ' ἂν αὐτὸν ἴδοι μέγαν
γεγενημένον, οὐχὶ παρ' αὑτοῦ. ὧν οὖν ἐκεῖνος μὲν
ὀφείλει τοῖς ὑπὲρ αὑτοῦ πεπολιτευμένοις χάριν, ὑμῖν
δὲ δίκην προσήκει λαβεῖν, τούτων οὐχὶ νῦν ὁρῶ τὸν
10 καιρὸν τοῦ λέγειν. ἃ δὲ καὶ χωρὶς τούτων ἔνι, καὶ
βέλτιόν ἐστιν ἀκηκοέναι πάντας ὑμᾶς, καὶ μεγάλα,
ὦ ἄνδρες Ἀθηναῖοι, κατ' ἐκείνου φαίνοιτ' ἂν ὀνείδη
βουλομένοις ὀρθῶς δοκιμάζειν, ταῦτ' εἰπεῖν πειρά-
σομαι.

5   Τὸ μὲν οὖν ἐπίορκον καὶ ἄπιστον καλεῖν ἄνευ τοῦ
16 τὰ πεπραγμένα δεικνύναι λοιδορίαν εἶναι τις ἂν
φήσειε κενὴν δικαίως· τὸ δὲ πάνθ', ὅσα πώποτ'
ἔπραξε, διεξιόντα ἐφ' ἅπασι τούτοις ἐλέγχειν καὶ
βραχέος λόγου συμβαίνει δεῖσθαι, καὶ δυοῖν ἕνεκα
20 ἡγοῦμαι συμφέρειν εἰρῆσθαι, τοῦ τ' ἐκείνου, ὅπερ
καὶ ἀληθὲς ὑπάρχει, φαῦλον φαίνεσθαι, καὶ τοῦ
τοὺς ὑπερεκπεπληγμένους ὡς ἄμαχόν τινα τὸν Φίλιππον ἰδεῖν ὅτι πάντα διεξελήλυθεν οἷς πρότερον
παρακρουόμενος μέγας ηὐξήθη, καὶ πρὸς αὐτὴν ἥκει
6 τὴν τελευτὴν τὰ πράγματ' αὐτοῦ. ἐγὼ γάρ, ὦ ἄν-
26 δρες Ἀθηναῖοι, σφόδρ' ἂν ἡγούμην καὶ αὐτὸς φοβερὸν τὸν Φίλιππον καὶ θαυμαστόν, εἰ τὰ δίκαια

πράττοντα ἑώρων αὐτὸν ηὐξημένον· νῦν δὲ θεωρῶν.
καὶ σκοπῶν εὑρίσκω τὴν μὲν ἡμετέραν εὐήθειαν τὸ
κατ᾽ ἀρχάς, ὅτε Ὀλυνθίους ἀπήλαυνόν τινες ἐνθένδε
βουλομένους ἡμῖν διαλεχθῆναι, τῷ τὴν Ἀμφίπολιν
φάσκειν παραδώσειν καὶ τὸ θρυλούμενόν ποτε ἀπόρ- 5
ρητον ἐκεῖνο κατασκευάσαι, τούτῳ προσαγαγόμενον,
τὴν δ᾽ Ὀλυνθίων φιλίαν μετὰ ταῦτα τῷ Ποτίδαιαν 7
οὖσαν ὑμετέραν ἐξελεῖν καὶ τοὺς μὲν πρότερον συμμάχους ὑμᾶς ἀδικῆσαι, παραδοῦναι δὲ ἐκείνοις,
Θετταλοὺς δὲ νῦν τὰ τελευταῖα τῷ Μαγνησίαν 10
παραδώσειν ὑποσχέσθαι καὶ τὸν Φωκικὸν πόλεμον
πολεμήσειν ὑπὲρ αὐτῶν ἀναδέξασθαι. ὅλως δὲ
οὐδεὶς ἔστιν ὅντιν᾽ οὐ πεφενάκικεν ἐκεῖνος τῶν αὐτῷ
χρησαμένων· τὴν γὰρ ἑκάστων ἄνοιαν ἀεὶ τῶν ἀγ-
νοούντων αὐτὸν ἐξαπατῶν καὶ προσλαμβάνων οὕτως 15
ηὐξήθη. ὥσπερ οὖν διὰ τούτων ἤρθη μέγας, ἡνίκα 8
ἕκαστοι συμφέρον αὐτὸν ἑαυτοῖς ᾤοντό τι πράξειν,
οὕτως ὀφείλει διὰ τῶν αὐτῶν τούτων καὶ καθαιρεθῆναι πάλιν, ἐπειδὴ πάνθ᾽ ἕνεκα ἑαυτοῦ ποιῶν ἐξελή-
λεγκται. καιροῦ μὲν δή, ὦ ἄνδρες Ἀθηναῖοι, πρὸς 20
τοῦτο πάρεστι Φιλίππῳ τὰ πράγματα· ἢ παρελθών
τις ἐμοί, μᾶλλον δὲ ὑμῖν δειξάτω ὡς οὐκ ἀληθῆ
ταῦτ᾽ ἐγὼ λέγω, ἢ ὡς οἱ τὰ πρῶτα ἐξηπατημένοι
τὰ λοιπὰ πιστεύσουσιν, ἢ ὡς οἱ παρὰ τὴν αὐτῶν
ἀξίαν δεδουλωμένοι Θετταλοὶ νῦν οὐκ ἂν ἐλεύθεροι 25
γένοιντο ἄσμενοι.

Καὶ μὴν εἴ τις ὑμῶν ταῦτα μὲν οὕτως ἔχειν 9

ἡγεῖται, οἴεται δὲ βίᾳ καθέξειν αὐτὸν τὰ πράγματα
τῷ τὰ χωρία καὶ λιμένας καὶ τὰ τοιαῦτα προειλη-
φέναι, οὐκ ὀρθῶς οἴεται. ὅταν μὲν γὰρ ὑπ᾽ εὐνοίας
τὰ πράγματα συστῇ καὶ πᾶσι ταὐτὰ συμφέρῃ τοῖς
5 μετέχουσι τοῦ πολέμου, καὶ συμπονεῖν καὶ φέρειν
τὰς συμφορὰς καὶ μένειν ἐθέλουσιν ἄνθρωποι· ὅταν
δ᾽ ἐκ πλεονεξίας καὶ πονηρίας τις ὥσπερ οὗτος
ἰσχύσῃ, ἡ πρώτη πρόφασις καὶ μικρὸν πταῖσμα
10 ἅπαντα ἀνεχαίτισε καὶ διέλυσεν. οὐ γὰρ ἔστιν,
10 οὐκ ἔστιν, ὦ ἄνδρες Ἀθηναῖοι, ἀδικοῦντα καὶ ἐπιορ-
κοῦντα καὶ ψευδόμενον δύναμιν βεβαίαν κτήσασθαι,
ἀλλὰ τὰ τοιαῦτα εἰς μὲν ἅπαξ καὶ βραχὺν χρόνον
ἀντέχει, καὶ σφόδρα γε ἤνθησεν ἐπὶ ταῖς ἐλπίσιν,
ἂν τύχῃ, τῷ χρόνῳ δὲ φωρᾶται καὶ περὶ αὑτὰ κα-
15 ταρρεῖ. ὥσπερ γὰρ οἰκίας, οἶμαι, καὶ πλοίου καὶ
τῶν ἄλλων τῶν τοιούτων τὰ κάτωθεν ἰσχυρότατα
εἶναι δεῖ, οὕτω καὶ τῶν πράξεων τὰς ἀρχὰς καὶ
τὰς ὑποθέσεις ἀληθεῖς καὶ δικαίας εἶναι προσήκει. τοῦτο δὲ οὐκ ἔνι νῦν ἐν τοῖς πεπραγμένοις
20 Φιλίππῳ.

11   Φημὶ δὴ δεῖν ὑμᾶς τοῖς μὲν Ὀλυνθίοις βοηθεῖν,
καὶ ὅπως τις λέγει κάλλιστα καὶ τάχιστα, οὕτως
ἀρέσκει μοι· πρὸς δὲ Θετταλοὺς πρεσβείαν πέμπειν, ἢ τοὺς μὲν διδάξει ταῦτα, τοὺς δὲ παροξυνεῖ·
25 καὶ γὰρ νῦν εἰσὶν ἐψηφισμένοι Παγασὰς ἀπαιτεῖν
12 καὶ περὶ Μαγνησίας λόγους ποιεῖσθαι. σκοπεῖσθε
μέντοι τοῦτο, ὦ ἄνδρες Ἀθηναῖοι, ὅπως μὴ λόγους

ἐροῦσι μόνον οἱ παρ' ἡμῶν πρέσβεις, ἀλλὰ καὶ
ἔργον τι δεικνύειν ἕξουσιν ἐξεληλυθότων ἡμῶν ἀξίως
τῆς πόλεως καὶ ὄντων ἐπὶ τοῖς πράγμασιν, ὡς ἅπας
μὲν λόγος, ἂν ἀπῇ τὰ πράγματα, μάταιόν τι φαίνε-
ται καὶ κενόν, μάλιστα δὲ ὁ παρὰ τῆς ἡμετέρας πό- 5
λεως· ὅσῳ γὰρ ἑτοιμότατ' αὐτῷ δοκοῦμεν χρῆσθαι,
τοσούτῳ μᾶλλον ἀπιστοῦσι πάντες αὐτῷ. πολλὴν 13
δὴ τὴν μετάστασιν καὶ μεγάλην δεικτέον τὴν μετα-
βολὴν, εἰσφέροντας, ἐξιόντας, ἅπαντα ποιοῦντας
ἑτοίμως, εἴπερ τις ὑμῖν προσέξει τὸν νοῦν. κἂν 10
ταῦτα ἐθελήσητε ὡς προσήκει καὶ δεῖ περαίνειν, οὐ
μόνον, ὦ ἄνδρες Ἀθηναῖοι, τὰ συμμαχικὰ ἀσθενῶς
καὶ ἀπίστως ἔχοντα φανήσεται Φιλίππῳ, ἀλλὰ καὶ
τὰ τῆς οἰκείας ἀρχῆς καὶ δυνάμεως κακῶς ἔχοντα
ἐξελεγχθήσεται. 15

Ὅλως μὲν γὰρ ἡ Μακεδονικὴ δύναμις καὶ ἀρχὴ 14
ἐν μὲν προσθήκης μέρει ἐστί τις οὐ μικρά, οἷον
ὑπῆρξέ ποθ' ὑμῖν ἐπὶ Τιμοθέου πρὸς Ὀλυνθίους·
πάλιν αὖ πρὸς Ποτίδαιαν Ὀλυνθίοις ἐφάνη τι τοῦτο
συναμφότερον· νυνὶ δὲ Θετταλοῖς στασιάζουσι καὶ 20
τεταραγμένοις ἐπὶ τὴν τυραννικὴν οἰκίαν ἐβοήθησε·
καὶ ὅποι τις ἄν, οἶμαι, προσθῇ κἂν μικρὰν δύναμιν,
πάντ' ὠφελεῖ. αὐτὴ δὲ καθ' αὑτὴν ἀσθενὴς καὶ
πολλῶν κακῶν ἐστὶ μεστή. καὶ γὰρ οὗτος ἅπασι 15
τούτοις οἷς ἄν τις μέγαν αὐτὸν ἡγήσαιτο, τοῖς πολέ- 25
μοις καὶ ταῖς στρατείαις, ἔτ' ἐπισφαλεστέραν ἢ
ὑπῆρχε φύσει κατεσκεύακεν ἑαυτῷ. μὴ γὰρ οἴεσθε,

ὦ ἄνδρες Ἀθηναῖοι, τοῖς αὐτοῖς Φίλιππόν τε χαίρειν
καὶ τοὺς ἀρχομένους, ἀλλ᾽ ὁ μὲν δόξης ἐπιθυμεῖ καὶ
τοῦτο ἐζήλωκε, καὶ προῄρηται πράττων καὶ κινδυ-
νεύων, ἂν συμβῇ τι, παθεῖν, τὴν τοῦ διαπράξασθαι
5 ταῦτα ἃ μηδεὶς πώποτε ἄλλος Μακεδόνων βασιλεὺς
16 δόξαν ἀντὶ τοῦ ζῆν ἀσφαλῶς ᾑρημένος· τοῖς δὲ τῆς
μὲν φιλοτιμίας τῆς ἀπὸ τούτων οὐ μέτεστι, κοπτόμενοι δὲ ἀεὶ ταῖς στρατείαις ταύταις ταῖς ἄνω κάτω
λυποῦνται καὶ συνεχῶς ταλαιπωροῦσιν οὔτ᾽ ἐπὶ τοῖς
10 ἔργοις οὔτ᾽ ἐπὶ τοῖς αὑτῶν ἰδίοις ἐώμενοι διατρίβειν,
οὔθ᾽ ὅσ᾽ ἂν πορίσωσιν οὕτως ὅπως ἂν δύνωνται, ταῦτ᾽
ἔχοντες διαθέσθαι κεκλειμένων τῶν ἐμπορίων τῶν ἐν
17 τῇ χώρᾳ διὰ τὸν πόλεμον.　οἱ μὲν οὖν πολλοὶ Μακεδόνων πῶς ἔχουσι Φιλίππῳ, ἐκ τούτων ἄν τις σκέ-
15 ψαιτο οὐ χαλεπῶς· οἱ δὲ δὴ περὶ αὐτὸν ὄντες ξένοι
καὶ πεζέταιροι δόξαν μὲν ἔχουσιν ὡς εἰσὶ θαυμαστοὶ
καὶ συγκεκροτημένοι τὰ τοῦ πολέμου, ὡς δ᾽ ἐγὼ
τῶν ἐν αὐτῇ τῇ χώρᾳ γεγενημένων τινὸς ἤκουον, ἀν-
δρὸς οὐδαμῶς οἵου τε ψεύδεσθαι, οὐδένων εἰσὶ βελ-
18 τίους.　εἰ μὲν γάρ τις ἀνήρ ἐστιν ἐν αὐτοῖς οἷος
21 ἔμπειρος πολέμου καὶ ἀγώνων, τούτους μὲν φιλοτι-
μίᾳ πάντας ἀπωθεῖν αὐτὸν ἔφη, βουλόμενον πάντα
αὑτοῦ δοκεῖν εἶναι τὰ ἔργα (πρὸς γὰρ αὖ τοῖς ἄλλοις καὶ τὴν φιλοτιμίαν ἀνυπέρβλητον εἶναι)· εἰ
25 δέ τις σώφρων ἢ δίκαιος ἄλλως, τὴν καθ᾽ ἡμέραν
ἀκρασίαν τοῦ βίου καὶ μέθην καὶ κορδακισμοὺς οὐ
δυνάμενος φέρειν, παρεῶσθαι καὶ ἐν οὐδενὸς εἶναι

μέρει τὸν τοιοῦτον. λοιποὺς δὴ περὶ αὐτὸν εἶναι 19
λῃστὰς καὶ κόλακας καὶ τοιούτους ἀνθρώπους οἵους
μεθυσθέντας ὀρχεῖσθαι τοιαῦτα οἷα ἐγὼ νῦν ὀκνῶ
πρὸς ὑμᾶς ὀνομάσαι. δῆλον δ' ὅτι ταῦτ' ἐστὶν
ἀληθῆ· καὶ γὰρ οὓς ἐνθένδε πάντες ἀπήλαυνον ὡς 5
πολὺ τῶν θαυματοποιῶν ἀσελγεστέρους ὄντας, Καλλίαν ἐκεῖνον τὸν δημόσιον καὶ τοιούτους ἀνθρώπους,
μίμους γελοίων καὶ ποιητὰς αἰσχρῶν ᾀσμάτων ὧν
εἰς τοὺς συνόντας ποιοῦσιν ἕνεκα τοῦ γελασθῆναι,
τούτους ἀγαπᾷ καὶ περὶ αὑτὸν ἔχει. καίτοι ταῦτα, 20
εἰ καὶ μικρά τις ἡγεῖται, μεγάλα, ὦ ἄνδρες Ἀθη- 11
ναῖοι, δείγματα τῆς ἐκείνου γνώμης καὶ κακοδαιμονίας ἐστὶ τοῖς εὖ φρονοῦσιν. ἀλλ', οἶμαι, νῦν μὲν
ἐπισκοτεῖ τούτοις τὸ κατορθοῦν· αἱ γὰρ εὐπραξίαι
δειναὶ συγκρύψαι τὰ τοιαῦτα ὀνείδη· εἰ δέ τι 15
πταίσει, τότ' ἀκριβῶς αὐτοῦ ταῦτ' ἐξετασθήσεται.
δοκεῖ δ' ἔμοιγε, ὦ ἄνδρες Ἀθηναῖοι, δείξειν οὐκ εἰς
μακράν, ἂν οἵ τε θεοὶ θέλωσι καὶ ὑμεῖς βούλησθε.
ὥσπερ γὰρ ἐν τοῖς σώμασιν, τέως μὲν ἂν ἐρρωμέ- 21
νος ᾖ τις, οὐδὲν ἐπαισθάνεται, ἐπὰν δὲ ἀρρώστημά 20
τι συμβῇ, πάντα κινεῖται, κἂν ῥῆγμα κἂν στρέμμα
κἂν ἄλλο τι τῶν ὑπαρχόντων σαθρὸν ᾖ, οὕτω καὶ
τῶν πόλεων καὶ τῶν τυράννων, ἕως μὲν ἂν ἔξω πο-
λεμῶσιν, ἀφανῆ τὰ κακὰ τοῖς πολλοῖς ἐστίν, ἐπειδὰν δὲ ὅμορος πόλεμος συμπλακῇ, πάντα ἐποίησεν 25
ἔκδηλα.

Εἰ δέ τις ὑμῶν, ὦ ἄνδρες Ἀθηναῖοι, τὸν Φίλιπ- 22

B

πον εὐτυχοῦντα ὁρῶν ταύτῃ φοβερὸν προσπολεμῆ-
σαι νομίζει, σώφρονος μὲν ἀνθρώπου λογισμῷ
χρῆται· μεγάλη γὰρ ῥοπή, μᾶλλον δὲ τὸ ὅλον ἡ
τύχη παρὰ πάντ᾽ ἐστὶ τὰ τῶν ἀνθρώπων πράγ-
5 ματα· οὐ μὴν ἀλλ᾽ ἔγωγε, εἴ τις αἵρεσίν μοι δοίη,
τὴν τῆς ἡμετέρας πόλεως τύχην ἂν ἑλοίμην, ἐθε-
λόντων ἃ προσήκει ποιεῖν ὑμῶν αὐτῶν καὶ κατὰ
μικρόν, ἢ τὴν ἐκείνου· πολὺ γὰρ πλείους ἀφορμὰς
εἰς τὸ τὴν παρὰ τῶν θεῶν εὔνοιαν ἔχειν ὁρῶ ἡμῖν
23 ἐνούσας ἢ ἐκείνῳ. ἀλλ᾽ οἶμαι, καθήμεθα οὐδὲν
11 ποιοῦντες· οὐκ ἔνι δ᾽ αὐτὸν ἀργοῦντα οὐδὲ τοῖς
φίλοις ἐπιτάττειν ὑπὲρ αὐτοῦ τι ποιεῖν, μή τί γε
δὴ τοῖς θεοῖς. οὐ δὴ θαυμαστόν ἐστιν εἰ στρατευό-
μενος καὶ πονῶν ἐκεῖνος αὐτὸς καὶ παρὼν ἐφ᾽ ἅπασι
15 καὶ μηδένα καιρὸν μηδ᾽ ὥραν παραλείπων ἡμῶν
μελλόντων καὶ ψηφιζομένων καὶ πυνθανομένων
περιγίγνεται. οὐδὲ θαυμάζω τοῦτ᾽ ἐγώ· τοὐναντίον γὰρ ἂν ἦν θαυμαστόν, εἰ μηδὲν ποιοῦντες ἡμεῖς
ὧν τοῖς πολεμοῦσι προσήκει τοῦ πάντα ποιοῦντος
24 περιῆμεν. ἀλλ᾽ ἐκεῖνο θαυμάζω, εἰ Λακεδαιμονίοις
21 μέν ποτε, ὦ ἄνδρες Ἀθηναῖοι, ὑπὲρ τῶν Ἑλληνικῶν
δικαίων ἀντήρατε, καὶ πολλὰ ἰδίᾳ πλεονεκτῆσαι
πολλάκις ὑμῖν ἐξὸν οὐκ ἠθελήσατε, ἀλλ᾽ ἵν᾽ οἱ ἄλλοι
τύχωσι τῶν δικαίων, τὰ ὑμέτερ᾽ αὐτῶν ἀνηλίσκετε
25 εἰσφέροντες καὶ προεκινδυνεύετε στρατευόμενοι, νυνὶ
δ᾽ ὀκνεῖτε ἐξιέναι καὶ μέλλετε εἰσφέρειν ὑπὲρ τῶν
ὑμετέρων αὐτῶν κτημάτων, καὶ τοὺς μὲν ἄλλους

σεσώκατε πολλάκις πάντας καὶ καθ᾽ ἕνα αὐτῶν
ἕκαστον ἐν μέρει, τὰ δ᾽ ὑμέτερ᾽ αὐτῶν ἀπολωλεκό-
τες κάθησθε. ταῦτα θαυμάζω, καὶ ἔτι πρὸς τού-25
τοις εἰ μηδὲ εἷς ὑμῶν, ὦ ἄνδρες Ἀθηναῖοι, δύναται
λογίσασθαι πόσον πολεμεῖτε χρόνον Φιλίππῳ, καὶ 5
τί ποιούντων ὑμῶν ὁ χρόνος διελήλυθεν οὗτος. ἴστε
γὰρ δήπου τοῦθ᾽, ὅτι μελλόντων αὐτῶν, ἑτέρους
τινὰς ἐλπιζόντων πράξειν, αἰτιωμένων ἀλλήλους,
κρινόντων, πάλιν ἐλπιζόντων, σχεδὸν ταὐτὰ ἅπερ
νυνὶ ποιούντων ἅπας ὁ χρόνος διελήλυθεν. εἶθ᾽ 26
οὕτως ἀγνωμόνως ἔχετε, ὦ ἄνδρες Ἀθηναῖοι, ὥστε 11
δι᾽ ὧν ἐκ χρηστῶν φαῦλα τὰ πράγματα τῆς πόλεως
γέγονε, διὰ τούτων ἐλπίζετε τῶν αὐτῶν πράξεων ἐκ
φαύλων αὐτὰ χρηστὰ γενήσεσθαι; ἀλλ᾽ οὔτ᾽ εὔλο-
γον οὔτ᾽ ἔχον ἐστὶ φύσιν τοῦτό γε· πολὺ γὰρ ῥᾷον 15
ἔχοντας φυλάττειν ἢ κτήσασθαι πάντα πέφυκεν.
νυνὶ δὲ ὅ τι μὲν φυλάξομεν, οὐδέν ἐστιν ὑπὸ τοῦ
πολέμου λοιπὸν τῶν πρότερον, κτήσασθαι δὲ δεῖ.
αὐτῶν οὖν ἡμῶν ἔργον τοῦτ᾽ ἤδη. φημὶ δὴ δεῖν εἰσφέ-27
ρειν χρήματα, αὐτοὺς ἐξιέναι προθύμως, μηδέν᾽ αἰτιᾶ-20
σθαι πρὶν ἂν τῶν πραγμάτων κρατήσητε, τηνικαῦτα
δὲ ἀπ᾽ αὐτῶν τῶν ἔργων κρίναντας τοὺς μὲν ἀξίους
ἐπαίνου τιμᾶν, τοὺς δ᾽ ἀδικοῦντας κολάζειν, τὰς προφάσεις δ᾽ ἀφελεῖν καὶ τὰ καθ᾽ ὑμᾶς ἐλλείμματα·
οὐ γὰρ ἔστι πικρῶς ἐξετάσαι τί πέπρακται τοῖς 25
ἄλλοις, ἂν μὴ παρ᾽ ὑμῶν αὐτῶν πρῶτον ὑπάρξῃ τὰ
δέοντα. τίνος γὰρ ἕνεκα, ὦ ἄνδρες Ἀθηναῖοι, νομί-28

ζετε τοῦτον μὲν φεύγειν τὸν πόλεμον πάντας ὅσους
ἂν ἐκπέμψητε στρατηγούς, ἰδίους δ' εὑρίσκειν πο-
λέμους, εἰ δεῖ τι τῶν ὄντων καὶ περὶ τῶν στρατη-
γῶν εἰπεῖν. ὅτι ἐνταῦθα μέν ἐστι τὰ ἆθλα, ὑπὲρ ὧν
5 ἐστὶν ὁ πόλεμος, ὑμέτερα· Ἀμφίπολις κἂν ληφθῇ,
παραχρῆμα αὐτὴν ὑμεῖς κομιεῖσθε· οἱ δὲ κίνδυνοι
τῶν ἐφεστηκότων ἴδιοι, μισθὸς δ' οὐκ ἔστιν· ἐκεῖ δὲ
κίνδυνοι μὲν ἐλάττους, τὰ δὲ λήμματα τῶν ἐφεστηκότων καὶ τῶν στρατιωτῶν, Λάμψακος, Σίγειον, τὰ
10 πλοῖα ἃ συλῶσιν. ἐπ' οὖν τὸ λυσιτελοῦν αὐτοῖς
29 ἕκαστοι χωροῦσιν. ὑμεῖς δέ, ὅταν μὲν εἰς τὰ
πράγματα ἀποβλέψητε φαύλως ἔχοντα, τοὺς ἐφε-
στηκότας κρίνετε, ὅταν δὲ δόντες λόγον τὰς ἀνάγκας
ἀκούσητε ταύτας, ἀφίετε. περίεστι τοίνυν ὑμῖν
15 ἀλλήλοις ἐρίζειν καὶ διεστάναι, τοῖς μὲν ταῦτα
πεπεισμένοις, τοῖς δὲ ταῦτα, τὰ κοινὰ δ' ἔχειν φαύλως. πρότερον μὲν γάρ, ὦ ἄνδρες Ἀθηναῖοι, εἰσε-
φέρετε κατὰ συμμορίας, νυνὶ δὲ πολιτεύεσθε κατὰ
συμμορίας. ῥήτωρ ἡγεμὼν ἑκατέρων, καὶ στρατη-
20 γὸς ὑπὸ τούτῳ, καὶ οἱ βοησόμενοι τριακόσιοι· οἱ
δ' ἄλλοι προσνενέμησθε οἳ μὲν ὡς τούτους, οἳ δὲ
30 ὡς ἐκείνους. δεῖ δὴ ταῦτα ἐπανέντας καὶ ὑμῶν
αὐτῶν ἔτι καὶ νῦν γενομένους κοινὸν καὶ τὸ λέγειν
καὶ τὸ βουλεύεσθαι καὶ τὸ πράττειν ποιῆσαι. εἰ δὲ
25 τοῖς μὲν ὥσπερ ἐκ τυραννίδος ὑμῶν ἐπιτάττειν ἀποδώσετε, τοῖς δ' ἀναγκάζεσθαι τριηραρχεῖν, εἰσφέρειν,
στρατεύεσθαι, τοῖς δὲ ψηφίζεσθαι κατὰ τούτων μό-

νον, ἄλλο δὲ μηδ' ὁτιοῦν συμπονεῖν, οὐχὶ γενήσεται
τῶν δεόντων ὑμῖν οὐδὲν ἐν καιρῷ· τὸ γὰρ ἠδικημένον
ἀεὶ μέρος ἐλλείψει, εἶθ' ὑμῖν τούτους κολάζειν ἀντὶ
τῶν ἐχθρῶν περιέσται. λέγω δὴ κεφάλαιον, πάντας §1
εἰσφέρειν ἀφ' ὅσων ἕκαστος ἔχει, τὸ ἴσον· πάντας 5
ἐξιέναι κατὰ μέρος, ἕως ἂν ἅπαντες στρατεύσησθε·
πᾶσι τοῖς παριοῦσι λόγον διδόναι, καὶ τὰ βέλτιστα
ὧν ἂν ἀκούσητε αἱρεῖσθαι, μὴ ἃ ἂν ὁ δεῖνα ἢ ὁ
δεῖνα εἴπῃ. κἂν ταῦτα ποιῆτε, οὐ τὸν εἰπόντα
μόνον παραχρῆμα ἐπαινέσεσθε, ἀλλὰ καὶ ὑμᾶς 10
αὐτοὺς ὕστερον, βέλτιον τῶν ὅλων πραγμάτων ὑμῖν
ἐχόντων.

ΟΛΥΝΘΙΑΚΟΣ Γ.

1 Οὐχὶ ταὐτὰ παρίσταταί μοι γιγνώσκειν, ὦ ἄνδρες Ἀθηναῖοι, ὅταν τε εἰς τὰ πράγματα ἀποβλέψω
καὶ ὅταν πρὸς τοὺς λόγους οὓς ἀκούω· τοὺς μὲν
γὰρ λόγους περὶ τοῦ τιμωρήσασθαι Φίλιππον ὁρῶ
5 γιγνομένους, τὰ δὲ πράγματα εἰς τοῦτο προήκοντα
ὥστε ὅπως μὴ πεισόμεθα αὐτοὶ πρότερον κακῶς
σκέψασθαι δέον. οὐδὲν οὖν ἄλλο μοι δοκοῦσιν οἱ
τὰ τοιαῦτα λέγοντες ἢ τὴν ὑπόθεσιν, περὶ ἧς βου-
λεύεσθε, οὐχὶ τὴν οὖσαν παριστάντες ὑμῖν ἁμαρτά-
2 νειν. ἐγὼ δ᾽ ὅτι μέν ποτ᾽ ἐξῆν τῇ πόλει καὶ τὰ
11 αὑτῆς ἔχειν ἀσφαλῶς καὶ Φίλιππον τιμωρήσασθαι,
καὶ μάλα ἀκριβῶς οἶδα· ἐπ᾽ ἐμοῦ γάρ, οὐχὶ πάλαι
γέγονε ταῦτα ἀμφότερα· νῦν μέντοι πέπεισμαι
τοῦθ᾽ ἱκανὸν προλαβεῖν ἡμῖν εἶναι τὴν πρώτην, ὅπως
15 τοὺς συμμάχους σώσομεν. ἐὰν γὰρ τοῦτο βεβαίως
ὑπάρξῃ, τότε καὶ περὶ τοῦ τίνα τρόπον τιμωρήσεταί
τις ἐκεῖνον ἐξέσται σκοπεῖν· πρὶν δὲ τὴν ἀρχὴν
ὀρθῶς ὑποθέσθαι, μάταιον ἡγοῦμαι περὶ τῆς τελευ-
τῆς ὁντινοῦν ποιεῖσθαι λόγον.

3 Ὁ μὲν οὖν παρὼν καιρός, ὦ ἄνδρες Ἀθηναῖοι,
21 εἴπερ ποτέ, πολλῆς φροντίδος καὶ βουλῆς δεῖται·
ἐγὼ δὲ οὐχ ὅ τι χρὴ περὶ τῶν παρόντων συμβου-

λεῦσαι χαλεπώτατον ἡγοῦμαι, ἀλλ' ἐκεῖν' ἀπορῶ,
τίνα χρὴ τρόπον, ὦ ἄνδρες Ἀθηναῖοι, πρὸς ὑμᾶς
περὶ αὐτῶν εἰπεῖν. πέπεισμαι γὰρ ἐξ ὧν παρὼν
καὶ ἀκούων σύνοιδα, τὰ πλείω τῶν πραγμάτων ὑμᾶς
ἐκπεφευγέναι τῷ μὴ βούλεσθαι τὰ δέοντα ποιεῖν ἢ 5
τῷ μὴ συνιέναι. ἀξιῶ δὲ ὑμᾶς, ἂν μετὰ παρρησίας
ποιῶμαι τοὺς λόγους, ὑπομένειν, τοῦτο θεωροῦντας εἰ
τἀληθῆ λέγω, καὶ διὰ τοῦτο, ἵνα τὰ λοιπὰ βελτίω
γένηται· ὁρᾶτε γὰρ ὡς ἐκ τοῦ πρὸς χάριν δημηγορεῖν
ἐνίους εἰς πᾶν προελήλυθε μοχθηρίας τὰ παρόντα. 10

Ἀναγκαῖον δὲ ὑπολαμβάνω μικρὰ τῶν γεγενημέ- 4
νων πρῶτον ὑμᾶς ὑπομνῆσαι. μέμνησθε, ὦ ἄνδρες
Ἀθηναῖοι, ὅτ' ἀπηγγέλθη Φίλιππος ὑμῖν ἐν Θρᾴκῃ
τρίτον ἢ τέταρτον ἔτος τουτὶ Ἡραῖον τεῖχος πολιορ-
κῶν. τότε τοίνυν μὴν μὲν ἦν μαιμακτηριών, πολ- 15
λῶν δὲ λόγων καὶ θορύβου γιγνομένου παρ' ὑμῖν
ἐψηφίσασθε τετταράκοντα τριήρεις καθέλκειν καὶ
τοὺς μέχρι πέντε καὶ τετταράκοντα ἐτῶν αὐτοὺς ἐμ-
βαίνειν καὶ τάλαντα ἑξήκοντα εἰσφέρειν. καὶ μετὰ 5
ταῦτα διελθόντος τοῦ ἐνιαυτοῦ τούτου ἑκατομβαιῶν, 20
μεταγειτνιῶν, βοηδρομιών· τούτου τοῦ μηνὸς μόγις
μετὰ τὰ μυστήρια δέκα ναῦς ἀπεστείλατε ἔχοντα
κενὰς Χαρίδημον καὶ πέντε τάλαντα ἀργυρίου. ὡς
γὰρ ἠγγέλθη Φίλιππος ἀσθενῶν ἢ τεθνεώς (ἦλθε
γὰρ ἀμφότερα), οὐκέτι καιρὸν οὐδένα τοῦ βοηθεῖν 25
νομίσαντες ἀφεῖτε, ὦ ἄνδρες Ἀθηναῖοι, τὸν ἀπόστο-
λον. ἦν δ' οὗτος ὁ καιρὸς αὐτός· εἰ γὰρ τότε

ἐκεῖσε ἐβοηθήσαμεν, ὥσπερ ἐψηφισάμεθα, προθύμως, οὐκ ἂν ἠνώχλει νῦν ἡμῖν ὁ Φίλιππος σωθείς.

6 Τὰ μὲν δὴ τότε πραχθέντα οὐκ ἂν ἄλλως ἔχοι·
νῦν δ᾽ ἑτέρου πολέμου καιρὸς ἥκει τις, δι᾽ ὃν καὶ
5 περὶ τούτων ἐμνήσθην, ἵνα μὴ ταὐτὰ πάθητε. τί
δὴ χρησόμεθα, ὦ ἄνδρες Ἀθηναῖοι, τούτῳ; εἰ γὰρ
μὴ βοηθήσετε παντὶ σθένει κατὰ τὸ δυνατόν, θεάσασθε ὃν τρόπον ὑμεῖς ἐστρατηγηκότες πάντα
7 ἔσεσθε ὑπὲρ Φιλίππου. ὑπῆρχον Ὀλύνθιοι δύνα-
10 μίν τινα κεκτημένοι, καὶ διέκειθ᾽ οὕτω τὰ πράγματα·
οὔτε Φίλιππος ἐθάρρει τούτους οὔθ᾽ οὗτοι Φίλιππον.
ἐπράξαμεν ἡμεῖς κἀκεῖνοι πρὸς ἡμᾶς εἰρήνην· ἦν
τοῦτο ὥσπερ ἐμπόδισμά τι τῷ Φιλίππῳ καὶ δυσχερές, πόλιν μεγάλην ἐφορμεῖν τοῖς ἑαυτοῦ καιροῖς
15 διηλλαγμένην πρὸς ἡμᾶς. ἐκπολεμῶσαι δεῖν ᾠόμεθα
τοὺς ἀνθρώπους ἐκ παντὸς τρόπου· καὶ ὃ πάντες
8 ἐθρύλουν, τοῦτο πέπρακται νυνὶ ὁπωσδήποτε. τί
οὖν ὑπόλοιπον, ὦ ἄνδρες Ἀθηναῖοι, πλὴν βοηθεῖν
ἐρρωμένως καὶ προθύμως; ἐγὼ μὲν οὐχ ὁρῶ· χωρὶς
20 γὰρ τῆς περιστάσης ἂν ἡμᾶς αἰσχύνης εἰ καθυφεί-
μεθά τι τῶν πραγμάτων, οὐδὲ τὸν φόβον, ὦ ἄνδρες
Ἀθηναῖοι, μικρὸν ὁρῶ τὸν τῶν μετὰ ταῦτα, ἐχόντων
μὲν ὡς ἔχουσι Θηβαίων ἡμῖν, ἀπειρηκότων δὲ χρή-
μασι Φωκέων, μηδενὸς δ᾽ ἐμποδὼν ὄντος Φιλίππῳ
25 τὰ παρόντα καταστρεψαμένῳ πρὸς ταῦτα ἐπικλῖ-
9 ναι τὰ πράγματα. ἀλλὰ μὴν εἴ τις ὑμῶν εἰς τοῦτο
ἀναβάλλεται ποιήσειν τὰ δέοντα, ἰδεῖν ἐγγύθεν βού-

λεται τὰ δεινά, ἐξὸν ἀκούειν ἄλλοθι γιγνόμενα, καὶ
βοηθοὺς ἑαυτῷ ζητεῖν, ἐξὸν νῦν ἑτέροις αὐτὸν βοη-
θεῖν· ὅτι γὰρ εἰς τοῦτο περιστήσεται τὰ πράγματα
ἐὰν τὰ παρόντα προώμεθα, σχεδὸν ἴσμεν ἅπαντες
δήπου.   5

   Ἀλλ' ὅτι μὲν δὴ δεῖ βοηθεῖν, εἴποι τις ἄν, πάν- 10
τες ἐγνώκαμεν, καὶ βοηθήσομεν· τὸ δὲ ὅπως, τοῦτο
λέγε. μὴ τοίνυν, ὦ ἄνδρες Ἀθηναῖοι, θαυμάσητε
ἂν παράδοξον εἴπω τι τοῖς πολλοῖς. νομοθέτας
καθίσατε. ἐν δὲ τούτοις τοῖς νομοθέταις μὴ θῆσθε 10
νόμον μηδένα (εἰσὶ γὰρ ἱκανοὶ ὑμῖν), ἀλλὰ τοὺς εἰς
τὸ παρὸν βλάπτοντας ὑμᾶς λύσατε. λέγω δὲ τοὺς 11
περὶ τῶν θεωρικῶν, σαφῶς οὑτωσί, καὶ τοὺς περὶ
τῶν στρατευομένων ἐνίους, ὧν οἱ μὲν τὰ στρατιωτικὰ τοῖς οἴκοι μένουσι διανέμουσι θεωρικά, οἱ δὲ 15
τοὺς ἀτακτοῦντας ἀθῴους καθιστᾶσιν, εἶτα καὶ τοὺς
τὰ δέοντα ποιεῖν βουλομένους ἀθυμοτέρους ποιοῦσιν. ἐπειδὰν δὲ ταῦτα λύσητε καὶ τὴν τοῦ τὰ βέλτιστα λέγειν ὁδὸν παράσχητε ἀσφαλῆ, τηνικαῦτα
τὸν γράψοντα ἃ πάντες ἴστε ὅτι συμφέρει ζητεῖτε. 20
πρὶν δὲ ταῦτα πρᾶξαι, μὴ σκοπεῖτε τίς εἰπὼν τὰ 12
βέλτιστα ὑπὲρ ὑμῶν ὑφ' ὑμῶν ἀπολέσθαι βουλήσε-
ται· οὐ γὰρ εὑρήσετε, ἄλλως τε καὶ τούτου μόνου
περιγίγνεσθαι μέλλοντος, παθεῖν ἀδίκως τι κακὸν
τὸν ταῦτ' εἰπόντα καὶ γράψαντα, μηδὲν δὲ ὠφελῆ- 25
σαι τὰ πράγματα, ἀλλὰ καὶ εἰς τὸ λοιπὸν μᾶλλον
ἔτι ἢ νῦν τὸ τὰ βέλτιστα λέγειν φοβερώτερον·

ποιῆσαι. καὶ λύειν γε, ὦ ἄνδρες Ἀθηναῖοι, τοὺς
νόμους δεῖ τούτους τοὺς αὐτοὺς ἀξιοῦν οἵπερ καὶ
13 τεθείκασιν· οὐ γάρ ἐστι δίκαιον τὴν μὲν χάριν, ἣ
πᾶσαν ἔβλαψε τὴν πόλιν, τοῖς τότε θεῖσιν ὑπάρ-
5 χειν, τὴν δ' ἀπέχθειαν, δι' ἧς ἂν ἅπαντες ἄμεινον
πράξαιμεν, τῷ νῦν τὰ βέλτιστα εἰπόντι ζημίαν γενέσθαι. πρὶν δὲ ταῦτα εὐτρεπίσαι, μηδαμῶς, ὦ
ἄνδρες Ἀθηναῖοι, μηδένα ἀξιοῦτε τηλικοῦτον εἶναι
παρ' ὑμῖν ὥστε τοὺς νόμους τούτους παραβάντα μὴ
10 δοῦναι δίκην, μηδ' οὕτως ἀνόητον ὥστε εἰς προὖπτον
κακὸν αὐτὸν ἐμβαλεῖν.

14 Οὐ μὴν οὐδ' ἐκεῖνό γ' ὑμᾶς ἀγνοεῖν δεῖ, ὦ ἄνδρες
Ἀθηναῖοι, ὅτι ψήφισμα οὐδενὸς ἄξιόν ἐστιν, ἂν μὴ
προσγένηται τὸ ποιεῖν ἐθέλειν τά γε δόξαντα προ-
15 θύμως ὑμᾶς. εἰ γὰρ αὐτάρκη τὰ ψηφίσματα ἦν ἢ
ὑμᾶς ἀναγκάζειν ἃ προσήκει πράττειν ἢ περὶ ὧν ἂν
γραφῇ διαπράξασθαι, οὔτ' ἂν ὑμεῖς πολλὰ ψηφιζό-
μενοι μικρά, μᾶλλον δ' οὐδὲν ἐπράττετε τούτων,
οὔτε Φίλιππος τοσοῦτον ὑβρίκει χρόνον· πάλαι γὰρ
15 ἂν ἕνεκά γε ψηφισμάτων ἐδεδώκει δίκην. ἀλλ' οὐχ
21 οὕτω ταῦτ' ἔχει· τὸ γὰρ πράττειν τοῦ λέγειν καὶ
χειροτονεῖν ὕστερον ὂν τῇ τάξει, πρότερον τῇ δυνά-
μει καὶ κρεῖττόν ἐστίν. τοῦτ' οὖν δεῖ προσεῖναι,
τὰ δ' ἄλλα ὑπάρχει· καὶ γὰρ εἰπεῖν τὰ δέοντα
25 παρ' ὑμῖν εἰσιν, ὦ ἄνδρες Ἀθηναῖοι, δυνάμενοι, καὶ
γνῶναι πάντων ὑμεῖς ὀξύτατοι τὰ ῥηθέντα, καὶ
16 πρᾶξαι δὲ δυνήσεσθε νῦν, ἐὰν ὀρθῶς ποιῆτε. τίνα

γὰρ χρόνον ἢ τίνα καιρὸν, ὦ ἄνδρες Ἀθηναῖοι, τοῦ
παρόντος βελτίω ζητεῖτε; ἢ πότε ἃ δεῖ πράξετε, εἰ
μὴ νῦν; οὐχ ἅπαντα μὲν ἡμῶν προείληφε τὰ χωρία
ἄνθρωπος, εἰ δὲ καὶ ταύτης κύριος τῆς χώρας γενήσεται, πάντων αἴσχιστα πεισόμεθα; οὐχ οὕς, εἰ 5
πολεμήσαιεν, ἑτοίμως σώσειν ὑπισχνούμεθα, οὗτοι
νῦν πολεμοῦνται; οὐκ ἐχθρός; οὐκ ἔχων τὰ ἡμέτερα; οὐ βάρβαρος; οὐχ ὅ τι ἂν εἴποι τις; ἀλλὰ 17
πρὸς θεῶν πάντα ἐάσαντες καὶ μόνον οὐχὶ συγκα-
τασκευάσαντες αὐτῷ τότε τοὺς αἰτίους, οἵτινές εἰσι, 10
τούτων ζητήσομεν; οὐ γὰρ αὐτοί γ' αἴτιοι φήσομεν
εἶναι, σαφῶς οἶδα τοῦτ' ἐγώ. οὐδὲ γὰρ ἐν τοῖς τοῦ
πολέμου κινδύνοις τῶν φυγόντων οὐδεὶς ἑαυτοῦ
κατηγορεῖ, ἀλλὰ τοῦ στρατηγοῦ καὶ τῶν πλησίον
καὶ πάντων μᾶλλον, ἥττηνται δ' ὅμως διὰ πάντας 15
τοὺς φυγόντας δήπου· μένειν γὰρ ἐξῆν τῷ κατηγο-
ροῦντι τῶν ἄλλων, εἰ δὲ τοῦτ' ἐποίει ἕκαστος,
ἐνίκων ἄν. καὶ νῦν οὐ λέγει τις τὰ βέλτιστα· 18
ἀναστὰς ἄλλος εἰπάτω, μὴ τοῦτον αἰτιάσθω. ἕτερος λέγει τις βελτίω· ταῦτα ποιεῖτε ἀγαθῇ τύχῃ. 20
ἀλλ' οὐχ ἡδέα ταῦτα· οὐκέτι τοῦθ' ὁ λέγων ἀδικεῖ,
πλὴν εἰ δέον εὔξασθαι παραλείπει. εὔξασθαι μὲν
γάρ, ὦ ἄνδρες Ἀθηναῖοι, ῥᾴδιον, εἰς ταὐτὸ πάνθ'
ὅσα βούλεταί τις ἀθροίσαντα ἐν ὀλίγῳ· ἑλέσθαι δέ,
ὅταν περὶ πραγμάτων προτεθῇ σκοπεῖν, οὐκέθ' 25
ὁμοίως εὔπορον, ἀλλὰ δεῖ τὰ βέλτιστα ἀντὶ τῶν
ἡδέων, ἂν μὴ συναμφότερα ἐξῇ, λαμβάνειν. εἰ δέ 19

τις ἡμῖν ἔχει καὶ τὰ θεωρικὰ ἐᾶν καὶ πόρους ἑτέρους
λέγειν στρατιωτικούς, οὐχ οὗτος κρείττων; εἴποι
τις ἄν. φήμ' ἔγωγε, εἴπερ ἔστιν, ὦ ἄνδρες Ἀθηναῖοι·
ἀλλὰ θαυμάζω εἴ τῳ ποτὲ ἀνθρώπων ἢ γέγονεν ἢ
5 γενήσεται, ἂν τὰ παρόντα ἀναλώσῃ πρὸς ἃ μὴ δεῖ,
τῶν ἀπόντων εὐπορῆσαι πρὸς ἃ δεῖ. ἀλλ' οἶμαι,
μέγα τοῖς τοιούτοις ὑπάρχει λόγοις ἡ παρ' ἑκάστου
βούλησις, διόπερ ῥᾷστον ἁπάντων ἐστὶν αὑτὸν
ἐξαπατῆσαι· ὃ γὰρ βούλεται, τοῦθ' ἕκαστος καὶ
10 οἴεται, τὰ δὲ πράγματα πολλάκις οὐχ οὕτω πέφυκεν.
20 ὁρᾶτε οὖν, ὦ ἄνδρες Ἀθηναῖοι, ταῦθ' οὕτως, ὅπως
καὶ τὰ πράγματα ἐνδέχεται, καὶ δυνήσεσθε ἐξιέναι
καὶ μισθὸν ἕξετε. οὔ τοι σωφρόνων οὐδὲ γενναίων
ἐστὶν ἀνθρώπων, ἐλλείποντάς τι δι' ἔνδειαν χρημά-
15 των τῶν τοῦ πολέμου εὐχερῶς τὰ τοιαῦτα ὀνείδη
φέρειν, οὐδ' ἐπὶ μὲν Κορινθίους καὶ Μεγαρέας ἁρπά-
σαντας τὰ ὅπλα πορεύεσθαι, Φίλιππον δ' ἐᾶν πόλεις Ἑλληνίδας ἀνδραποδίζεσθαι δι' ἀπορίαν ἐφο-
δίων τοῖς στρατευομένοις.

21 Καὶ ταῦτ' οὐχ ἵν' ἀπέχθωμαί τισιν ὑμῶν τὴν
21 ἄλλως προῄρημαι λέγειν· οὐ γὰρ οὕτως ἄφρων οὐδ'
ἀτυχής εἰμι ἐγὼ ὥστε ἀπεχθάνεσθαι βούλεσθαι
μηδὲν ὠφελεῖν νομίζων· ἀλλὰ δικαίου πολίτου
κρίνω τὴν τῶν πραγμάτων σωτηρίαν ἀντὶ τῆς ἐν
25 τῷ λέγειν χάριτος αἱρεῖσθαι. καὶ γὰρ τοὺς ἐπὶ
τῶν προγόνων ἡμῶν λέγοντας ἀκούω, ὥσπερ ἴσως
καὶ ὑμεῖς, οὓς ἐπαινοῦσι μὲν οἱ παριόντες ἅπαντες

μιμοῦνται δ' οὐ πάνυ, τούτῳ τῷ ἔθει καὶ τῷ τρόπῳ
τῆς πολιτείας χρῆσθαι, τὸν Ἀριστείδην ἐκεῖνον,
τὸν Νικίαν, τὸν ὁμώνυμον ἐμαυτῷ, τὸν Περι-
κλέα. ἐξ οὗ δ' οἱ διερωτῶντες ὑμᾶς οὗτοι πεφή- 22
νασι ῥήτορες "τί βούλεσθε; τί γράψω; τί ὑμῖν 5
χαρίσωμαι;" προπέποται τῆς παραυτίκα χάριτος
τὰ τῆς πόλεως πράγματα καὶ τοιαυτὶ συμβαίνει,
καὶ τὰ μὲν τούτων πάντα καλῶς ἔχει, τὰ δ'
ὑμέτερα αἰσχρῶς. καίτοι σκέψασθε, ὦ ἄνδρες 23
Ἀθηναῖοι, ἅ τις ἂν κεφάλαια εἰπεῖν ἔχοι τῶν τ' ἐπὶ 10
τῶν προγόνων ἔργων καὶ τῶν ἐφ' ὑμῶν. ἔσται δὲ
βραχὺς καὶ γνώριμος ὑμῖν ὁ λόγος· οὐ γὰρ ἀλλοτρίοις ὑμῖν χρωμένοις παραδείγμασιν ἀλλ' οἰκείοις,
ὦ ἄνδρες Ἀθηναῖοι, εὐδαίμοσιν ἔξεστι γενέσθαι.
ἐκεῖνοι τοίνυν, οἷς οὐκ ἐχαρίζονθ' οἱ λέγοντες οὐδ' 24
ἐφίλουν αὐτοὺς ὥσπερ ὑμᾶς οὗτοι νῦν, πέντε μὲν 16
καὶ τετταράκοντα ἔτη τῶν Ἑλλήνων ἦρξαν ἑκόντων, πλείω δ' ἢ μύρια τάλαντα εἰς τὴν ἀκρόπολιν
ἀνήγαγον, ὑπήκουε δὲ ὁ ταύτην τὴν χώραν ἔχων
αὐτοῖς βασιλεὺς ὥσπερ ἐστὶ προσῆκον βάρβαρον 20
Ἕλλησι, πολλὰ δὲ καὶ καλὰ καὶ πεζῇ καὶ ναυμα-
χοῦντες ἔστησαν τρόπαια αὐτοὶ στρατευόμενοι, μό-
νοι δὲ ἀνθρώπων κρείττω τὴν ἐπὶ τοῖς ἔργοις δόξαν
τῶν φθονούντων κατέλιπον. ἐπὶ μὲν δὴ τῶν Ἑλ- 25
ληνικῶν ἦσαν τοιοῦτοι· ἐν δὲ τοῖς κατὰ τὴν πόλιν 25
αὐτὴν θεάσασθε ὁποῖοι, ἔν τε τοῖς κοινοῖς καὶ ἐν
τοῖς ἰδίοις. δημοσίᾳ μὲν τοίνυν οἰκοδομήματα καὶ

κάλλη τοιαῦτα καὶ τοσαῦτα κατεσκεύασαν ἡμῖν
ἱερῶν καὶ τῶν ἐν τούτοις ἀναθημάτων ὥστε μηδενὶ
26 τῶν ἐπιγιγνομένων ὑπερβολὴν λελεῖφθαι· ἰδίᾳ δ'
οὕτω σώφρονες ἦσαν καὶ σφόδρα ἐν τῷ τῆς πολι-
5 τείας ἤθει μένοντες ὥστε τὴν Ἀριστείδου καὶ τὴν
Μιλτιάδου καὶ τῶν τότε λαμπρῶν οἰκίαν εἴ τις ἄρα
οἶδεν ὑμῶν ὁποία ποτ' ἐστίν, ὁρᾷ τῆς τοῦ γείτονος
οὐδὲν σεμνοτέραν οὖσαν· οὐ γὰρ εἰς περιουσίαν
ἐπράττετο αὐτοῖς τὰ τῆς πόλεως, ἀλλὰ τὸ κοινὸν
10 αὔξειν ἕκαστος ᾤετο δεῖν. ἐκ δὲ τοῦ τὰ μὲν Ἑλλη-
νικὰ πιστῶς, τὰ δὲ πρὸς τοὺς θεοὺς εὐσεβῶς, τὰ δ'
ἐν αὑτοῖς ἴσως διοικεῖν μεγάλην εἰκότως ἐκτήσαντο
27 εὐδαιμονίαν. τότε μὲν δὴ τοῦτον τὸν τρόπον εἶχε
τὰ πράγματα ἐκείνοις, χρωμένοις οἷς εἶπον προστά-
15 ταις· νυνὶ δὲ πῶς ὑμῖν ὑπὸ τῶν χρηστῶν τῶν νῦν
τὰ πράγματα ἔχει; ἀρά γε ὁμοίως καὶ παραπλησίως; τὰ μὲν ἄλλα σιωπῶ, πόλλ' ἂν ἔχων
εἰπεῖν· ἀλλ' ὅσης ἅπαντες ὁρᾶτε ἐρημίας ἐπειλημ-
μένοι, καὶ Λακεδαιμονίων μὲν ἀπολωλότων, Θη-
20 βαίων δ' ἀσχόλων ὄντων, τῶν δ' ἄλλων οὐδενὸς
ὄντος ἀξιόχρεω περὶ τῶν πρωτείων ἡμῖν ἀντιτάξα-
σθαι, ἐξὸν δ' ἡμῖν καὶ τὰ ἡμέτερ' αὐτῶν ἀσφαλῶς
28 ἔχειν καὶ τὰ τῶν ἄλλων δίκαια βραβεύειν, ἀπεστερήμεθα μὲν χώρας οἰκείας, πλείω δ' ἢ χίλια καὶ
25 πεντακόσια τάλαντα ἀνηλώκαμεν εἰς οὐδὲν δέον,
οὓς δ' ἐν τῷ πολέμῳ συμμάχους ἐκτησάμεθα, εἰρή-
νης οὔσης ἀπολωλέκασιν οὗτοι, ἐχθρὸν δ' ἐφ' ἡμᾶς

αὐτοὺς τηλικοῦτον ἠσκήκαμεν. ἢ φρασάτω τις ἐμοὶ
παρελθών, πόθεν ἄλλοθεν ἰσχυρὸς γέγονεν ἢ παρ᾽
ἡμῶν αὐτῶν Φίλιππος. ἀλλ᾽ ὦ τᾶν, εἰ ταῦτα 29
φαύλως, τά γ᾽ ἐν αὐτῇ τῇ πόλει νῦν ἄμεινον ἔχει.
καὶ τί ἂν εἰπεῖν τις ἔχοι; τὰς ἐπάλξεις ἃς κονιῶμεν, 5
καὶ τὰς ὁδοὺς ἃς ἐπισκευάζομεν, καὶ κρήνας, καὶ
λήρους; ἀποβλέψατε δὴ πρὸς τοὺς ταῦτα πολι-
τευομένους, ὧν οἱ μὲν ἐκ πτωχῶν πλούσιοι γεγό-
νασιν, οἱ δ᾽ ἐξ ἀδόξων ἔντιμοι, ἔνιοι δὲ τὰς ἰδίας
οἰκίας τῶν δημοσίων οἰκοδομημάτων σεμνοτέρας εἰσὶ 10
κατεσκευασμένοι, ὅσῳ δὲ τὰ τῆς πόλεως ἐλάττω
γέγονε, τοσούτῳ τὰ τούτων ηὔξηται.

Τί δὴ τὸ πάντων αἴτιον τούτων, καὶ τί δή ποτε 30
ἅπαντ᾽ εἶχε καλῶς τότε καὶ νῦν οὐκ ὀρθῶς; ὅτι τὸ
μὲν πρῶτον καὶ στρατεύεσθαι τολμῶν αὐτὸς ὁ δῆ- 15
μος δεσπότης τῶν πολιτευομένων ἦν καὶ κύριος
αὐτὸς ἁπάντων τῶν ἀγαθῶν, καὶ ἀγαπητὸν ἦν παρὰ
τοῦ δήμου τῶν ἄλλων ἑκάστῳ καὶ τιμῆς καὶ ἀρχῆς
καὶ ἀγαθοῦ τινὸς μεταλαβεῖν· νῦν δὲ τοὐναντίον 31
κύριοι μὲν οἱ πολιτευόμενοι τῶν ἀγαθῶν, καὶ διὰ 20
τούτων ἅπαντα πράττεται, ὑμεῖς δ᾽ ὁ δῆμος ἐκνενευρισμένοι καὶ περιῃρημένοι χρήματα καὶ συμμάχους
ἐν ὑπηρέτου καὶ προσθήκης μέρει γεγένησθε, ἀγαπῶντες ἐὰν μεταδιδῶσι θεωρικῶν ὑμῖν ἢ Βοηδρόμια
πέμψωσιν οὗτοι, καὶ τὸ πάντων ἀνδρειότατον, τῶν 25
ὑμετέρων αὐτῶν χάριν προσοφείλετε. οἱ δ᾽ ἐν αὐτῇ
τῇ πόλει καθείρξαντες ὑμᾶς ἐπάγουσιν ἐπὶ ταῦτα

32 καὶ τιθασεύουσι χειροήθεις αὐτοῖς ποιοῦντες. ἔστι
δ᾽ οὐδέποτ᾽, οἶμαι, μέγα καὶ νεανικὸν φρόνημα
λαβεῖν μικρὰ καὶ φαῦλα πράττοντας· ὁποῖ᾽ ἄττα
γὰρ ἂν τὰ ἐπιτηδεύματα τῶν ἀνθρώπων ᾖ, τοιοῦτον
5 ἀνάγκη καὶ τὸ φρόνημα ἔχειν. ταῦτα μὰ τὴν Δή-
μητρα οὐκ ἂν θαυμάσαιμι, εἰ μείζων εἰπόντι ἐμοὶ
γένοιτο παρ᾽ ὑμῶν βλάβη τῶν πεποιηκότων αὐτὰ
γενέσθαι· οὐδὲ γὰρ παρρησία περὶ πάντων ἀεὶ παρ᾽
ὑμῖν ἐστιν, ἀλλ᾽ ἔγωγε ὅτι καὶ νῦν γέγονε θαυμάζω.

33 Ἐὰν οὖν ἀλλὰ νῦν γ᾽ ἔτι ἀπαλλαγέντες τούτων
11 τῶν ἐθῶν ἐθελήσητε στρατεύεσθαί τε καὶ πράττειν
ἀξίως ὑμῶν αὐτῶν, καὶ ταῖς περιουσίαις ταῖς οἴκοι
ταύταις ἀφορμαῖς ἐπὶ τὰ ἔξω τῶν ἀγαθῶν χρήση-
σθε, ἴσως ἄν, ἴσως, ὦ ἄνδρες Ἀθηναῖοι, τέλειόν
15 τι καὶ μέγα κτήσαισθε ἀγαθόν, καὶ τῶν τοιούτων
λημμάτων ἀπαλλαγείητε, ἃ τοῖς ἀσθενοῦσι παρὰ
τῶν ἰατρῶν σιτίοις διδομένοις ἔοικε. καὶ γὰρ οὔτ᾽
ἰσχὺν ἐκεῖνα ἐντίθησιν οὔτ᾽ ἀποθνήσκειν ἐᾷ· καὶ
ταῦτα, ἃ νέμεσθε νῦν ὑμεῖς, οὔτε τοσαῦτά ἐστιν
20 ὥστε ὠφέλειαν ἔχειν τινὰ διαρκῆ, οὔτ᾽ ἀπογνόν-
τας ἄλλο τι πράττειν ἐᾷ, ἀλλ᾽ ἔστι ταῦτα τὴν
34 ἑκάστου ῥᾳθυμίαν ὑμῶν ἐπαυξάνοντα. οὐκοῦν σὺ
μισθοφορὰν λέγεις; φήσει τις. καὶ παραχρῆμά
γε τὴν αὐτὴν σύνταξιν ἁπάντων, ὦ ἄνδρες Ἀθη-
25 ναῖοι, ἵνα τῶν κοινῶν ἕκαστος τὸ μέρος λαμβάνων, ὅτου δέοιτο ἡ πόλις, τοῦθ᾽ ὑπάρχοι. ἔξεστιν ἄγειν ἡσυχίαν· οἴκοι μένων βελτίων, τοῦ δι᾽

ἔνδειαν ἀνάγκῃ τι ποιεῖν αἰσχρὸν ἀπηλλαγμένος.
συμβαίνει τι τοιοῦτον οἷον καὶ τὰ νῦν· στρατιώτης
αὐτὸς ὑπάρχων ἀπὸ τῶν αὐτῶν τούτων λημμάτων,
ὥσπερ ἐστὶ δίκαιον ὑπὲρ τῆς πατρίδος. ἔστι τις
ἔξω τῆς ἡλικίας ἡμῶν· ὅσα οὗτος ἀτάκτως νῦν λαμ- 5
βάνων οὐκ ὠφελεῖ, ταῦτ᾽ ἐν ἴσῃ τάξει λαμβάνων,
πάντ᾽ ἐφορῶν καὶ διοικῶν ἃ χρὴ πράττεσθαι. ὅλως 35
δὲ οὔτ᾽ ἀφελὼν οὔτε προσθείς, πλὴν μικρὸν τὴν
ἀταξίαν ἀνελὼν εἰς τάξιν ἤγαγον τὴν πόλιν, τὴν
αὐτὴν τοῦ λαβεῖν, τοῦ στρατεύεσθαι, τοῦ δικάζειν, 10
τοῦ ποιεῖν τοῦθ᾽ ὅ τι καθ᾽ ἡλικίαν ἕκαστος ἔχοι καὶ
ὅτου καιρὸς εἴη, τάξιν ποιήσας. οὐκ ἔστιν ὅπου
μηδὲν ποιοῦσιν ἐγὼ τὰ τῶν ποιησόντων εἶπον ὡς
δεῖ νέμειν, οὐδ᾽ αὐτοὺς μὲν ἀργεῖν καὶ σχολάζειν
καὶ ἀπορεῖν, ὅτι δὲ οἱ τοῦ δεῖνος νικῶσι ξένοι, ταῦτα 15
πυνθάνεσθαι· ταῦτα γὰρ νυνὶ γίγνεται. καὶ οὐχὶ 36
μέμφομαι τὸν ποιοῦντά τι τῶν δεόντων ὑπὲρ ὑμῶν,
ἀλλὰ καὶ ὑμᾶς ὑπὲρ ὑμῶν αὐτῶν ἀξιῶ πράττειν
ταῦτα ἐφ᾽ οἷς ἑτέρους τιμᾶτε, καὶ μὴ παραχωρεῖν,
ὦ ἄνδρες Ἀθηναῖοι, τῆς τάξεως, ἣν ὑμῖν οἱ πρόγο- 20
νοι τῆς ἀρετῆς μετὰ πολλῶν καὶ καλῶν κινδύνων
κτησάμενοι κατέλιπον.

Σχεδὸν εἴρηκα ἃ νομίζω συμφέρειν· ὑμεῖς δ᾽
ἔλοισθε ὅ τι καὶ τῇ πόλει καὶ ἅπασι συνοίσειν ὑμῖν
μέλλει. 25

NOTES.

NOTES.

1. Page 1, line 1. πολλῶν, emphatic in position, is further emphasized by separation from χρημάτων and association with ἄν. C. 621. It is not necessary to suppose, with the Scholiast, that in χρημάτων there is a distinct allusion to the theoric fund; for the same phraseology is used not unfrequently by Greek authors (cf. Andoc. 2, 21; Thuc. 1, 33; Isoc. 13, 11), and a similar expression is common in English; but the fact that he would fain persuade them in this oration to relinquish that fund for the military service, at least, gives additional fitness and force to this introduction. Thucydides and Isocrates use πρό instead of ἀντί in the parallel passages just cited. — ὦ ἄνδρες Ἀθηναῖοι, the usual address of Demosthenes, who never omits the respectful ἄνδρες, *gentlemen*, although he sometimes, in reproof, leaves out the ὦ. — 2. **νομίζω**, *I am persuaded*, I consider it as an established fact, or characteristic. — 3. **περὶ ὧν** = περὶ τούτων περὶ ὧν, *touching these things about which you are deliberating.* — **ὅτε**, lit. *when, while* = quandoquidem; less causal than ἐπεί, less contingent than εἰ, and more complimentary than either. — 4. **ἐθέλειν**, *to be willing:* βουλομένων, *wishing, intending,* cf. Ol. 2, 23: ἂν οἵ τε θεοὶ θέλωσι καὶ ὑμεῖς βούλησθε, *if the gods will and you wish*, that is, *choose*, or *resolve.* βούλεσθαι implies choice after deliberation (cf. βουλή), hence said only of rational beings; ἐθέλειν, a natural instinct or inclination, hence sometimes used of animals and the inanimate creation. So Pillon, Greek Synonymes, after the old grammarians, though contrary to Buttmann. See in Yonge's Eng. Gr. Lex., Drisler's ed., 129, where this passage is quoted in proof. Compare also de Contr. 3: μὴ μόνον ταῦτ' ἀκούειν ἐθέλοντα, ἀλλὰ καὶ πράττειν βουλόμενον, *not only willing to hear, but also choosing*, or *resolving to act.* — 6. **ἐσκεμμένος**, *with*

previous preparation, ant. to ἐκ τοῦ παραχρῆμα, *extempore*. The former
was Demosthenes's usual way of speaking (Plut. Dem. 8), and he
doubtless means or includes himself in ἥκει τις ; hence the ind. denoting a matter of fact.   Demades, who spoke against Demosthenes
in the matter of Olynthus, was a ready extemporizer, and a popular
demagogue.   Hence our orator might well ask a hearing for his *well-
considered advice*, not less than the unpremeditated harangues of
others.   See Rehdantz in loc. — 7. ἀκούσαντες, not as Schäfer, the
protasis of ἂν λάβοιτε, but as Heslop, the complement or preliminary
of that verb.   The condition is implied in γάρ and expressed in ἐθέλειν ἀκούειν : *for* (if you are willing to hear) *not only in case some one
has come prepared with some useful advice would you listen and adopt
it.* — τύχης, pred. gen., εἶναι being understood.   The genitive denotes
property or characteristic : *I conceive it to belong to your fortune.*
C. 440, b ; Cu. 417 ; G. 169, 1 ; H. 568.*   The fortunateness (felici-
tas) of Athens implies the favor of the gods, and is a compliment frequently paid to the Athenians by Demosthenes.   Ol. 2, 22 ; Phil. 2,
12, et al. — 9. ἐξ ἁπάντων, *out of all*, sc. both the prepared and the
unpremeditated.   This exordium is justly admired for its brevity,
simplicity, and appropriateness.   It is at once complimentary, manly,
and patriotic, and happily unites self-respect with respect for the
hearers.

2. 11. οὖν, not inferential, simply marks the transition from the
exordium to the subject-matter of the oration. — 12. μόνον οὐχί,
only not = all but, *almost.* — φωνὴν ἀφιείς, *with audible voice.* —
ὅτι...φροντίζετε, *that you must take those affairs in hand in person, if
you care for their safety.*   Notice the emphatic separation of ἐκείνων,
those affairs of Olynthus, from πραγμάτων, and of αὐτοῖς, *in person*,
not by mercenaries, from ὑμῖν.   One MS. and a few editors read
αὑτῶν = *your own* safety.   But the best have αὐτῶν referring to
πραγμάτων.   Cf. Ol. 3, 24 : τὴν τῶν πραγμάτων σωτηρίαν. — 14. ἡμεῖς
...αὐτά, *but we seem to be conducting ourselves I know not how in
regard to them.*   ἡμεῖς instead of ὑμεῖς for politeness ; for the same
reason οὐκ οἶδ, κ. τ. λ., instead of πάνυ ὀλιγώρως ἔχειν, which Lucian
puts in its place in his burlesque of this exordium.   Jov. Trag. 15.
— 15. δή, est colligentis : est *igitur*.   Franke.   The γέ limits the
clause, and not merely the pronoun.   τά γ᾽ ἐμοὶ δοκοῦντα is strictly,

---

* The references are to the grammars of Crosby, Rev. Ed., 1871 ; Curtius,
Harper's ed., 1872 ; Goodwin, 1870 ; Hadley, 1860.

those at least which seem best to me, while τὰ ἐμοιγε δοκοῦντα would be, *those which seem best to me at least.* Cf. Phil. 3, 29 : ὡς γ᾿ ἐμοὶ δόκει. The difference, however, is in form and emphasis rather than in substance : *as to measures, then, those at least which seem best to me are in the first place* (μέν) *to vote the* (required) *succor and get it in readiness as quick as possible...and also* (δέ) *to send meanwhile* (implied in the pres. inf. πέμπειν) *an embassy which shall inform them of this action.* "Observe the aorist παρασκευάσασθαι and the present πέμπειν afterwards, as if the act of sending the embassy were continuous till the return of those who were sent" (Whiston), or till the arrival of the troops. — 17. ἐνθένδε, from Athens, that is, citizens, and not mercenaries hired abroad. — βοηθήσετε. So Bekk., Dind., Whis.; al. βοηθήσητε. C. 624, b ; Cu. 553 ; G. 217 ; H. 756 ; Madv. 123.* The fut. ind. after ὅπως denotes a certain and direct consequence ; the aor. subj. (πάθητε) a more remote and contingent result. Compare Whiston and Heslop in loc. — 18. πρότερον. B. C. 352, when Philip invaded Thrace, and the Athenians were greatly alarmed for their possessions. Grote 11, 428. — 3. Page 2, line 1. ὡς, causal, *as* in the sense of *since.* — δέος, pred., τοῦτο, subj. — 2. ἄνθρωπος, *the man,* sc. Philip. — πανοῦργος, *unscrupulous.* — δεινὸς χρῆσθαι, *and skilful* (lit. terrible) *to take advantage of circumstances.* — 4. ἀξιόπιστος, κ. τ. λ., *and* in his threats *he might be shown,* sc. by his treatment of others, *quite worthy to be believed.* — 5. τρέψηται, κ. τ. λ., *may turn and wrest to his own purposes some of our chief interests.* W. — 4. 7. Οὐ...ἐπιεικῶς, *not but that indeed fairly.* The sentiment of what follows is, that the very autocracy which makes Philip so formidable an enemy will be likely also to make him an object of suspicion to the Olynthians and others. — 9. ἕνα ὄντα, a single individual = *alone,* or *in his own person.* The idea of the clause is well expressed by Heslop : *his having everything in his sole power to publish or keep secret.* — 11. ταμίαν, *paymaster.* See in De Cor. 235–36 the contrast drawn out at length between Philip in the full and sole possession of the entire civil, military, and money power, and Demosthenes as the responsible adviser of the Athenian democracy. — 13. πολλῷ προέχει, *is a great advantage.* — 14. ἐναντίως ἔχει, *is adverse.* The reason for this is given in the next section, viz. it awakens suspicion and fear. — 5. 16. περὶ δόξης, *about glory.* — 17. ὑπὲρ...χώρας, *in defence of a portion of their territory.* περί, lit.

* Madvig's Syntax.

= around; ὑπέρ = over. Hence ὑπέρ usually expresses a nearer relation and interest. ὑπέρ is to be supplied with ἀναστάσεως, κ. τ. λ., in a somewhat different sense = to *ward off*, or *prevent*. Dem. and other orators often use ὑπέρ where the historians used περί. — 18. ἅ... τούς, double acc. C. 480, b; Cu. 402; G. 165; H. 555. — 19. Ἀμ-φιπολιτῶν, part. gen. after τούς. For the situation of Amphipolis and its importance to the Athenians, see Smith's Dic. of Geog. For the history of its capture by Philip, see Thirlwall, 5, 196; Grote, 11, 330. For Pydna, Thirl. 5, 197; Grote, 11, 333. According to the Scholiast, Philip banished the betrayers of Amphipolis, and put to death those of Pydna. While he was engaged in the siege of Amphipolis, Philip quieted the Athenians with the assurance that he intended to restore it to them in exchange for Pydna; but when he had taken it, he seized Pydna also, and kept both under the pretext that inasmuch as they had not given him Pydna, he was not bound to restore Amphipolis to them, — an act of duplicity quite characteristic of Philip. — 21. καὶ ὅλως, κ. τ. λ., *and generally, I think, a despotism is an object of mistrust to free states.* The article with each of these nouns generalizes it, that is, defines despotisms and free states as a *genus* or class. C. 522; Cu. 375; H. 529. The neuter predicate corresponds with this and emphasizes it. C. 507; Cu. 366; H. 522. Demosthenes often repeats this maxim in sentiment and spirit; compare especially Phil. 2, 21 – 23, where he says that too close alliances with despots are dangerous to free states, and warns the Messenians to cherish mistrust (ἀπιστία) as their only safeguard. — 22. ἄλλως τε κἂν = *especially if.* See Lexicon and Grammar for explanation of this meaning. — 6. 23. ἐγνωκότας = *convinced of.* — ἃ προσήκει, sc. gloriam majorum, Græciæ principatum, oppressis opitulandi consuetudinem, injurias Philippi, periculi magnitudinem. Wolf. — 24. ἐθελῆσαι, taken absolutely = *be ready for action.* Westermann makes the following infin. depend on it. But cf. Thuc. 5, 9. — 25. παροξυνθῆναι, *be provoked to indignation.* — 27. αὐτούς, see note on αὐτοῖς, 2, above. — P. 3, l. 1. λόγος = *argument*, or *plea;* σκῆψις = *pretext*, or *excuse.* — ἔθ’ with a negative = *no longer.* — ὑπολείπεται = left *remaining*, lit. left *under*, as a support. — 7. 2. ἐθρυλεῖτε ὡς, al. ἐθρύλουν τέως, but ἐθρυλεῖτε is the reading of the most and best MSS., and τέως is not only a mere conjecture, but very improbable as *here* used. Render: *what you were all talking*, viz. *that*, etc. — 3. ἐκπολεμῶσαι, *to stir up to war.*

ἐκ- in composition emphasizes the *change out of* peace into war. —
4. **καὶ ταῦθ'**, *and that too.* C. 491, c. — 4. **ὡς** emphasized by **ἄν** =
in such manner as. C. 621, e. Cf. πολλῶν ἄν, § 1. — 6. **σφαλεροὶ**
...**ἴσως**, *they would have been unstable allies, and would have been
thus resolved up to a certain point perhaps.* σφαλεροί, lit. ready to
fall away, *unstable*, opp. to βεβαίαν in the antithetic member = *stable.*
Observe also the emphatic position of these words in their respective
clauses. — 8. **πρὸς αὐτοὺς ἐγκλημάτων**, grounds of complaint relating
to themselves, i. e. *grievances of their own.* — 8. 10. **δή** = *then*,
marking the conclusion. — 11. **παραπεπτωκότα...ἀφεῖναι**, *to lose such
a providential opportunity*, lit., and preserving the figure, *to let slip
such an occasion as has fallen into* your hands. — 13. **βεβοηθηκότες**,
after having aided. "Demosthenes makes frequent allusion to this
expedition as one that reflected especial credit on Athens, 4, 17 ; 8,
74 ; 16, 14 ; 18, 99. Thirl. 5, 225 ; Grote, 11, 338." Heslop. —
παρῆσαν...ἐπὶ with the accus. = *ascended, appeared on.* Dem. every-
where else uses παριέναι (not παρεῖναι) in this sense. But παρεῖναι
occurs in other orators. — 16. **παρειχόμεθ'** and **εἶχετ'** imperf. to denote
a continued action or state ; **ἦτε ἀπηλλαγμένοι**, plup., a complete
and final deliverance. — 9. 20. **Πύδνα, κ. τ. λ.** As Grote observes
(11, 329), Dem. always names these cities in the order of their capture : Amphipolis, B. C. 358 ; Pydna, 357 ; Potidæa, 356 ; Methone
and Pagasæ, 354 - 3. — 21. **τἄλλα.** Perhaps a rhetorical flourish.
Grote, 11, 365. — **ἵνα μή...διατρίβω**, *not to waste time.* — 22. **ἔνι**,
emphatic. — **τῷ πρώτῳ** = *the first best.* So Westermann and Rehdantz.
Al. τῳ πρώτῳ = any one first. — 24. **αὐτοί**, *in person*, not with mercenaries. — **ῥᾴονι**, *more facile*, i. e. *tractable.* See Lid. & Scott. —
21. **νῦν δέ**, *but as it is.* — 26. **αὐτόματ'...σχήσειν καλῶς**, *take care
of itself.* — 27. **ἡμεῖς**, emphatic. — P. 4, l. 2. **νυνὶ δή**, *now, I say*,
resumptive, cf. § 8. — 2. **τις οὗτος ὁ**, emphatic, τις stating it generally, οὗτος specifying, and ὁ still further defining. — 10. 5. **ἔμοιγε
δοκεῖ**, cf. note 2. δοκεῖ has the personal subject τις instead of being
used impersonally. C. 573 ; Cu. 571 ; H. 777. — **ἄν**, in the conclusion of a hypothetical sentence ; it is repeated before ἔχειν. The condition is expressed by καταστάς (C. 635 ; Cu. 583 ; G. 226 ; H. 789),
after which λογιστής is pred. nom. = *if he would establish himself an
impartial judge*, lit. auditor, — the allusion being to the balancing
of an *account*, and being continued through this and the following
section. — 6. **ὑπηργμένων**, favors *freely* conferred, *beginning* in their

good-will. — 9. ἀπολωλεκέναι, sc. ἡμᾶς. — κατὰ τὸν πόλεμον, in the course of the war, sc. about Amphipolis. — 10. ἀμελείας, gen. of property, after θείη = set to the account of, or reckon as belonging to. — μήτε πάλαι, not long ago, but recently, so that there is still hope of recovery. — μήτε...τε, like Lat. neque...et. — 13. παρ' ἐκείνων, from them, lit. from near them, from their presence ; render, as a blessing proceeding from their good-will. — 11. 14. παρόμοιόν ἐστιν ὅπερ, it is much like what takes place. παρα- adds emphasis, lit. when laid alongside, it is a parallel case. — 17. λάθῃ, render by an adverb unconsciously, i. e. gradually and before he is aware. — συναναλώσε καί, he loses with it also, gnomic aorist parallel with the present ἔχει in the antithesis, but emphasizing the proverbial character of the saying. C. 606 ; Cu. 494 ; G. 205 ; H. 707. — 18. καὶ περὶ ...οὕτως, so also in regard to public affairs. — οὐδ' εἰ...μνημονεύουσι = καὶ εἰ...οὐ μνημονεύουσι. Rehdantz. Well rendered by Heslop, forget too any good thing that has come to them from the gods. — 20. πρός, in reference to = by ; for every previous event is judged by the final result. — 22. καὶ σφόδρα is emphatic, and emphasizes not only δεῖ, but φροντίσαι. Well rendered by Whiston : wherefore must we, and that vigorously, turn our thoughts to the future ; lit. what remains, sc. the succor of Olynthus. — 23. ταῦτ' ἐπανορθωσάμενοι, by amending this, sc. the future. This lofty political ethics, enforced by the logic of common-sense, and illustrated from the common affairs of life, is characteristic of our orator. — 12. 25. καὶ τούτους, these men also, sc. the Olynthians, as well as the Amphipolitans and others mentioned in §§ 8, 9. — 26. εἶτ' = and then, or and in consequence. — 27. τί...ἔσται, what will there be that any longer prevents. — P. 5, l. 1. ὅποι βούλεται, e. g. to Athens. Cf. §§ 15 and 25 below. — 3. δι' ὅν, through which. — 4. τὸ πρῶτον, κ. τ. λ. Observe the order of the captures, cf. note 9, and the rapidity of them pictured by the rapid succession of clauses. — 6. ἐπέβη, B. C. 353 - 2, Grote, 11, 408 ; Thirlwall, 2, 97, Am. ed. — 7. εὐτρεπίσας, having made ready. — πάνθ' ὅν...τρόπον, in short, the whole country at his pleasure. Heslop. — 8. ὥχετ' εἰς, he was off into. — ἐκβαλών, after expelling some, e. g. Cersobleptes. — 9. καταστήσας, e. g. Amadocus and Berisades, B. C. 352. — ἠσθένησε, he fell sick. — 12 - 14. τὰς...στρατείας, his expeditions against the Illyrians and Pæonians (B. C. 359 - 8, near the beginning of his reign) and against Arymbas (king of the Molossians in Epirus, B. C. 351, succeeded by Alexander, his nephew, and brother of Olympias, Philip's wife), *and whithersoever one might speak of* **=** *and ever so many others one might mention.*

14. 14. Τί οὖν τις ἂν εἴποι, *Why, then, some one may say, do you speak these things to us now ?* In order to prevent τίς from standing first in its clause, the best editors omit the comma after οὖν, supposing the whole to be spoken as one clause in the Greek, although in English we must make two. — 16. καὶ τὸ προίεσθαι, *both how hurtful it is to be throwing away one after another continually some of our interests, and the restless activity which Philip practises and lives with,* i. e. in which he finds his business and has his being. — 18. ὑφ' ἧς, *under the influence of which.* — 21. ἐγνωκὼς ἔσται, *shall have resolved.* — ἀντιληπτέον ἐρρωμένως, *must take hold vigorously.* — 22. εἰς... τελευτῆσαι, *to what end, pray, is it to be expected that these things will come ?* — ποτ' = *tandem.* — 15. 24. ἐκεῖθεν for ἐκεῖ. C. 704. — 27. τὸν αὐτὸν τρόπον is an emphatic anticipation of οὕτω, and ὥσπερ is correlative to both. — ῥαδίως, *thoughtlessly.* — P. 6, l. 1. ἐπὶ τοῖς μεγάλοις τόκοις, *at the high rates of interest* exacted of such borrowers, — sometimes as high as 3 per cent a month, 36 per cent a year. Boeckh. Pub. Econ. I. chap. 22. — 2. καὶ, emphatic = *even.* — ἀπέστησαν, gnomic aorist. Render, *I fear lest just as those who borrow money thoughtlessly at such high rates of interest, after having luxuriated in plenty for a short time, afterwards lose even their original estates, so also we shall be found to have enjoyed our ease at a great cost.* — 4. πολλὰ...ὧν, *many of the disagreeable things.* Heslop. ὧν, partitive gen. — ποιεῖν depends on εἰς ἀνάγκην ἔλθωμεν = ἀναγκασθῶμεν, with the additional idea of *becoming* necessitated, emphatic for ἀναγκασθῶμεν. Here again political warning is enforced by familiar illustrations from common life.

16. 9. παντός, gen. of property or characteristic, *is anybody's work.* Whiston. — ὑπέρ, see note § 5. — 13. ἐν ὀργῇ ποιεῖσθε, *visit with your displeasure.* — 14. μήν = *yet* in antithesis to μέν. — 15. ὑποστείλασθαι, *to suppress* my sentiments, lit. to furl or take down sails. — 17. 17. τοῖς πράγμασιν, *the interests at stake,* dat. after βοηθητητέον. So Heslop. Whiston says : *in the case.* But the former is preferable. — τὰς πόλεις, sc. in Chalcidice, Olynthus and its allies. — 22. μάταιος...γένηται, *be rendered fruitless.* — 18. εἴτε γὰρ...εἴτε, *for if, on the one hand, in case you ravage his country, he shall suffer this and reduce Olynthus, he will then easily come to the relief of his own territory ; or if, on the other hand, in case you only send aid to Olynthus, he, seeing things at home in no danger, shall press the siege,* *and keep close watch of things there, he will overcome the besieged by the lapse of time.* — 24. παραστήσεται, *bring over,* i. e. *reduce.* See Lex. L. & S. sub v. C. II. — 27. τοῖς πράγμασι, which Heslop translates *his opportunity* and Whiston *the situation,* I have ventured to render *things there.* The commentators remark the emphasis of meaning in the two kindred words προσκαθεδεῖται and προσεδρεύσει. Demosthenes is fond of such *pairs* of words. See examples in my note on Dem. de Cor. § 4, l. 14. — P. 7, l. 1. τῷ χρόνῳ. Observe the article, not merely *in time,* but *by means of the lapse of time. Mora obsidionis* is Wolf's version. — δή = *then,* in conclusion.

19. 3. περὶ χρημάτων πόρου, *in regard to ways and means.* — ἔστιν...ἔστιν, *you have money, gentlemen of Athens, you have money to an amount which no people in the world has for military purposes.* Such emphatic repetitions are frequent in Demosthenes. — οὕτως ὡς βούλεσθε, *in such ways as you please,* i. e. for your pleasures, sc. theatricals and festivals. — 8. ἀποδώσετε, *restore* to its original military use, from which it had been perverted. — 8, 9. οὐδενὸς...πόρου, *there is no need of additional means...or rather there is an entire want of all such means.* Observe the article with the second πόρου. — 10. σὺ γράφεις, *do you move.* Such a motion would have exposed him to impeachment according to the law of Eubulus. Thirl. 5, 300 ; Grote, 11, 466. — 20. 12. εἶναι στρατιωτικά, *and this* (theoric fund) *ought to be a war fund.* The force of δεῖν extends through the member, what Demosthenes thinks *ought* to be done being set in emphatic contrast with what the people actually *do.* Dindorf omits the whole clause ; Bekker brackets ταῦτ', and Heslop omits it. But the words are in all the MSS., and are retained by Whiston. — 13. τὴν αὐτήν, that is, the same persons who receive the money should do military duty. Then they could have the money, and at the same time the state have soldiers. — ὑμεῖς δέ, *but you receive it thus somehow without service — for your festivals.* — οὕτω...πραγμάτων here = οὕτως...βούλεσθε above. — 16. εἰσφέρειν, make extraordinary contributions. The εἰσφορά was a special war tax. See Smith's Dic. Antiq. sub v. — 17. δεῖ δὲ χρημάτων, *but there is a necessity for money,* that is, money must be had. — 19. ἄλλους, other than an extraordinary contribution. ἄλλους ἄλλοι, *some one way* of raising money, *and some another.* — ἀντιλάβεσθε, κ. τ. λ., cf. note on ἀντιληπτέον, 14.

21. οὔτε...ἔχει, al. ἔχοι, but that is to be supplied. ἔχει goes with εὐτρεπῶς as well as with ὡς κάλλιστ', *for neither are things at present*

*in good trim as they appear to be, and as one might say that they are
without careful examination, nor in the best state they might be for
him.* The **οὐδ'** in the last clause is not correlative with **οὔτε** at the
beginning; it only adds a co-ordinate, but emphatic negative clause,
C. 701, c; Cu. 625, obs.; H. 859, a; and the **οὔτε** finds its correlative in the **οὔτ' ἂν ἐξήνεγκε** : *nor would he ever have engaged in this
war,* lit. carried it out. — 27. **ὡς ἐπιών,** elliptical for *ὡς ἐπιὼν ἀναιρεῖ-
ται* = primo statim impetu, *on the first advance.* — P. 8, l. 1. **ἀναιρήσεσθαι,** *to carry all before him.* — **κἄτα διέψευσται,** *and therein he
finds himself mistaken.* — 3. **γεγονός** denotes the cause of Philip's
trouble, *by* or *because of its having turned out contrary to expectation.*
— 22. 4. **ταῦτα,** sc. the character and conduct of the Thessalians.
The neuter pronoun is used to comprehend *all that pertains* to the
Thessalians. See Franke in loc. The Thessalians were proverbially
fickle and faithless. Cf. contra Aristoc., where Demosthenes says,
that while the Athenians never betrayed any of their friends, there
was none of *theirs* that the *Thessalians* did *not* betray. See also the
disorder and license imputed to the Thessalians by Socrates. Crit.
Cap. XV. — 5. **δήπου,** *you know.* **καί** connects *φύσει* and *ἀεί, by nature and always.* **κομιδῇ δέ** instead of *ἄπιστα δέ* correlative to *ἄπιστα
μέν,* hence the dative *τούτῳ.* — 8. **κεκωλύκασι,** *by their remonstrances.*
Cf. Ol. 2, 11, where the fact seems to be stated with more exactness.
Cf. Thirl. 5, 306; Grote, 11, 425. — **ἤκουον** as imperfect denotes a
continued or repeated hearing. — 9. **οὐδὲ...ἔτι,** *no longer,* as they *had*
permitted him to do since he ejected these tyrants. — 10. **καρποῦ-
σθαι,** lit. to harvest, that is, *to collect the revenues of.* — 11. **δέοι,** opt.
in or. obliqua, this being a part of what they said and he heard. —
ἀπό, *from,* i. e. by means of. — **λαμβάνειν,** pres. inf., *to be receiving.*
— 13. **κομιδῇ** = *πάνυ, altogether.* — **τὰ τῆς τροφῆς,** *the means of
support for his mercenaries.* — 23. 15. **ἁπλῶς...ἅπαντας,** *and all
these tribes generally.* — 17. **ἄνθρωπος,** *the man,* sc. Philip. — 18.
ὑβριστής, *tyrannical.* — 19. **ἴσως,** *perhaps.* Attic urbanity. — **τὸ
γὰρ, κ. τ. λ.** The idea is well expressed by Heslop : *for an undeserved
career of success becomes a source of folly to persons of weak mind.*
But there is a pith and point in the Greek, particularly in the antithesis between *εὖ πράττειν, doing well,* and *κακῶς φρονεῖν, thinking* or
planning ill, that is inevitably lost in a translation. This gnome
has been often quoted and much admired both for its form and its
sentiment; and the application of it in the next clause, *διόπερ, κ. τ. λ.,*

is still more striking. — 24. 23. τὴν ἀκαιρίαν...καιρόν, *the inopportune state of his affairs your opportunity.* Whiston cites as a parallel the saying of O'Connell: "England's need is Ireland's opportunity." — 24. συνάρασθαι, *to help* (the Olynthians) *in bearing the burdens of the war.* Whiston. — 25. ἐφ' ἃ δεῖ, *for all needful purposes.* — αὐτούς, *yourselves* in person. — 26. τοὺς ἄλλους, the other Greeks. — P. 9, l. 1. πῶς, a change from the indirect to the direct interrogation, which is more lively and spirited. — εἰ μηδ'...οὐ τολμήσετε. Here, too, the indirect question with which the sentence began seems to have given place to the more impassioned direct question ; for if the τολμήσετε followed regularly the εἰ and the οὐ were meant to be a mere repetition of the μηδ' for emphasis, μή would be required ; that is, the construction begins with εἰ and ends as if εἰ were not there : *Are you not ashamed, then, if not even what you would suffer if he had the power — will you not* (instead of *you will not*) *dare to do this when you have the opportunity ?* Observe the nice balancing of words in the antithesis of ποιῆσαι to πάθοιτ', and καιρὸν ἔχοντες to δύναιτ'.

25. 5. Ἔτι τοίνυν, *still further now.* — ἐκεῖ...ἐκεῖνον, in jenem lande...jener. Rehdantz. The *there* and *that man* are correlative. — 8. τὰ τῶν Ὀλυνθίων, nearly a periphrasis for *Olynthus.* C. 528 ; Cu. 410 ; G. 141, N. 4 ; Madv. 14 c : *if Olynthus* (or *the resources of the Olynthians*) *hold out* against him. — 9. τὴν ὑπάρχουσαν, κ. τ. λ., *this which you possess and which is your home,* sc. Attica. Whiston. — 10. ἀδεῶς, *without fear,* sc. of invasion by Philip. — 11. ἐκεῖνα = τὰ τῶν Ὀλυνθίων. — 26. 12. μὴ λίαν, κ. τ. λ., *I fear it may be too severe to say it, they will join with him in the invasion.* Cf. Plat. Gorg. 462 ε : μὴ ἀγροικότερον ᾖ τὸ ἀληθὲς εἰπεῖν. The truth, as Franke says, was even worse than he said, viz. that the Thebans would be the prime movers. Dindorf amends and reads οἱ εἰ μή, κ. τ. λ. — 15. ἀλλ' ὦ τᾶν, *but, my good sir, he* (Philip) *will not wish* (*choose*), sc. to march hither, — a remark supposed to be interjected by another, that the orator may answer it the more forcibly. — 16. τῶν ἀτοπωτάτων. "Neuter, 2, 2." Hes. "Masculinum est. Cf. 8, 58 ; 9, 14." Franke. ἄτοπος may be used of persons as well as things, see Lex., and the references, even that of Heslop, favor Franke's interpretation : *yet he would be one of the strangest of men.* And the protasis seems to require the same : εἰ...πράξει, *if what though incurring the reproach of folly thereby yet he talks out, this he will not do when he has the power.* Rehdantz calls εἰ μὴ...πράξει the

threatening ind. fut. — 27. 18. **ἡλίκα...ἥ,** *but how great the differences are between.* — 19. **προσδεῖν.** Observe the force of προσ-, the thing is so clear in itself as to require no argument *in addition.* — 21. **ἔξω,** *out of* the city. — 22. **χρωμένους λαμβάνειν.** Observe the present, *to be continually taking and using,* sc. during the month. τῶν is part. gen., *of the produce.* — 23. **λέγω,** *I mean.* — 25. **τὸν πρὸ τοῦ πόλεμον,** *the late war,* sc. the Amphipolitan, which lasted ten years and cost 1,500 talents. Ol. 3, 28. — **ζημιώσεσθαι** rem durantem indicat, **ζημιωθῆναι** (l. 24) rem unius momenti. Franke. The latter is the general statement, the former is more definite. For the fut. mid. instead of fut. pass. see Lex. C. 576 a ; Jelf 365, 6 a. — **προσέσθ',** *there is besides* (the loss of property) *the insult.* — P. 10, l. 1. **οὐδεμιᾶς, κ. τ. λ.,** *greater* (i. e. worse) *than any loss, at least in the view of sensible men.* Litotes. C. 686 i ; H. 665.

28. 3. **συνιδόντας,** *taking, then, all these things into consideration together, we ought all of us.* — 5. **καλῶς ποιοῦντες** may be rendered *fortunately, happily,* with Heslop and Kennedy, or *rightly, deservedly,* with Franke and L. & S., which see. Rüdiger : deorum benignitate, by the blessing of the gods. — 6. **τοὺς ἐν ἡλικίᾳ,** *those of age,* sc. to serve in the army, viz. from eighteen to sixty. — 9. **ἀκεραίου,** proleptic = *kept inviolate.* — **τοὺς δὲ λέγοντας,** *and the orators* (politicians) *that it may be easy for them to render an account of their administration since you will judge of their measures according to the state of your affairs, whatever it may be.* — 10. **εὔθυναι,** primarily of money ; here of measures. — 13. **παντὸς** is masc., acc. to Franke, Westermann, and the scholiast = *for the sake of every* citizen, i. e. the rich, the poor, etc., as above enumerated. But the more and better authorities make it neuter = *on every account ; and may they* (sc. τὰ πράγματα) *be prosperous on every account.* This oration, like that on the Crown and many others, closes with a prayer or wish for the well-being of his country. To begin with a prayer, as in the Or. de Cor., is less frequent. — **εἵνεκα,** al. **ἕνεκα,** Dem. seems sometimes to use the Ionic form of this word, perhaps for the sake of the rhythm. This peroration, or rather conclusion, which consists only of one section, and that a single sentence, is as simple and concise as the introduction. It is free from rhetorical display, and savors even more of the statesman than of the orator.

ΟΛΥΝΘΙΑΚΟΣ Β.

THE second Olynthiac opens in language and manner very like the first ; and Dindorf suggests that Dionysius, who cites the Orations by their opening words, has thus, by a slip of the memory, been led to confound them, and cite the second as the first. (See Introduction.)

1. Page 11, line 1. πολλῶν, emphatic as at the beginning of Ol. 1, where see note. ἄν with ἰδεῖν marks the conclusion of a hypothetical sentence (C. 618 ; Cu. 575 ; G. 211 ; H. 783), of which, however, the condition is omitted : *could see*, sc. if he would. C. 636 ; Cu. 544 ; G. 226, 2 ; H. 752. The structure of the sentence and the sentiment are quite similar to Ol. I. 10, where see notes particularly on δοκεῖ and παρά. Dem. is never weary of insisting on this topic, — the favor and good-will of the gods towards Athens. Cf. I. 1, and note there. — 2. γιγνομένην, *being continually manifested.* — 3. ἐν, not merely for variety (after ἐπὶ πολλῶν), but more exact and emphatic = not *at* or *on*, but *in*. — 4. τὸ γὰρ, κ. τ. λ., *for the fact that there have arisen those who are ready to wage war with Philip possessing both* (καὶ) *a neighboring country and some power and* (*what is most important of all*) *having their convictions about the war such as to think reconciliations with him to be in the first place untrustworthy and in the next ruinous to their country*, — *this is like some providential and altogether divine benefaction.* So Whiston. παντάπασιν, however, limits ἔοικεν, *is altogether like.* τινα = *some considerable.* δύναμιν = military power, *force.* In the Or. cont. Lept. the army of Olynthus about this time is stated at more than 10,000 hoplites and 1000 horse. διαλλαγάς here seems to differ from καταλλαγάς, Ol. 1, 4 (as Professor Champlin suggests), only as implying a *mutual* reconciliation, while there the orator is speaking expressly of the reconciliation *which Philip would gladly make with the Olynthians.* — 2. 11. αὑτούς, *ourselves*, in distinction from the gods, who are ready to help if we will help ourselves. — ὅπως, *how.* — 12. τῶν ὑπαρχόντων, *than our opportunities.* — αἰσχρῶν is usually considered as neuter and part. gen.; it could be masc. and gen. of property or characteristic : *it is the*

part of base men, nay, rather, of the basest. — 15. **φαίνεσθαι προϊεμέ-νους,** *to be seen continually giving up.* — **πόλεων** is explained by Rehdantz as part. gen.: *of the cities;* by most commentators as a case of inverted attraction to ὧν. — **τῆς τύχης** includes the divine favor. Cf. note, I. 1. This exordium is longer than that of the first Olynthiac, but not less simple, and more direct, launching more immediately in medias res. The religious idea is put in the foreground, and presented in an aspect which, while it is popular and conciliatory, furnishes also a strong incitement to duty.

3. 17. **μέν** is repeated by μέν, § 4, and both of them correspond to **ἃ δέ,** p. 12, l. 10. — **οὖν,** transitional, cf. Ol. 1, 2. — 21. **ὑπὲρ τού-των,** the strength of Philip in its various elements and parts. — **φιλο-τιμίαν,** *honor,* a secondary signification not confined to Demosthenes. L. & S. II. It suggests, however, the honor which results from an honor-seeking career. — 22. **οὐχὶ καλῶς,** litotes and euphemism for *dishonorably.* The use of ἡμῖν instead of ὑμῖν is in the same spirit. — **πλείονα ὑπὲρ τὴν ἀξίαν,** stronger than πλείονα ἢ κατ᾽ ἀξίαν, which would have been the regular construction : *more and greater things than could have been expected,* sc. of a king of Macedon. Cf. παρὰ τὴν ἀξίαν, 1. 23. — **4. 6. ἐνθένδ᾽,** made more emphatic by **ἂν** = *from this city and this bema.* — 7. **οὐχὶ παρ᾽ αὑτοῦ,** *not at all from himself.* The reader will observe the frequent recurrence of this emphatic form of the negative. — **ὧν οὖν, κ. τ. λ.** *Of the measures, therefore, for which he indeed owes a debt of gratitude to those who as public men have acted in his interest, but* (for which) *you ought to receive satisfaction, of these I do not now see the proper time to speak.* ὧν is gen. of crime, and τούτων gen. after καιρόν. τούτων is omitted by some of the best editors. — 10. **ἃ δέ, κ. τ. λ.,** *but what it is in my power to say quite* (καὶ) *irrespective of this,* etc. ἃ is object of λέγειν understood in the first clause and of ἀκηκοέναι in the second, and *subject* of φαίνοιτ᾽ in the third : *and what would be seen to be grounds of reproach to him if you were willing rightly to examine them.* **5. 17. δικαίως,** emphatic = *and justly so.* κενήν also is made emphatic by its position. — 18. **διεξιόντα...ἐλέγχειν** has τινά for subject, *but to rehearse all that he has ever done, and on the ground of all these acts to convict him,* sc. of being perjured and faithless. — καί, *both,* = *in the first place : in the first place happens to require only a short argument, and in the second place I think,* etc. — 20. **τοῦ τε...καὶ τοῦ,** appos. of δυοῖν = *both that ...and that.* — 22. **ὑπερεκπεπληγμένους,** *astonished at Philip,* more

3   D

frequently followed by ἐπί with dat. — 23. **διεξελήλυθεν**, run through
and so *exhausted all the arts of deception by which he formerly grew
to be great.* **παρακρούεσθαι**, lit. to cheat in weighing. *πρότερον*
limits both part. and verb. — **6.** Observe the separation for emphasis
of καὶ αὐτός from ἐγώ and σφόδρα from φοβερόν. — P. 13, l. 1. **πράττοντα**, *by doing.* The ethics of Dem. are always high-toned. — **θεωρῶν καὶ σκοπῶν**, *observing and examining.* Observe the pair of words
of kindred meaning so frequent in Dem. — 2-10. **τὴν μὲν ἡμετέραν**...
τὴν δ' Ὀλυνθίων...**Θετταλοὺς δέ,** *that he gained over* (προσαγαγόμενον)
in the first place (μέν) *our simplicity...in the second place the friendship
of the Olynthians...and now the Thessalians.* The *means* by which
each was gained is expressed by three clauses, each beginning with
τῷ. — **τὸ κατ' ἀρχάς**, *at the outset.* — **Ἀμφίπολιν**, cf. note, I. 4; Thirl.
5, 192; Grote 11, 328. — 5. **τὸ**...**ἀπόρρητον**, *by getting up* (lit. con-
structing, τῷ...κατασκευάσαι) *that secret article once so famous.* "The
Pydnæans being averse to this scheme (of transfer), it was alleged
that secrecy was essential to success, and consequently it was deter-
mined that the arrangement should be discussed before the senate
exclusively, and not before the assembly of the people" (Whiston).
6. **τούτῳ**, *by this means*, resumes and emphasizes the *means* expressed
in the foregoing clause. — 7. 7. **Ποτίδαιαν.** Cf. Thirl. 5, 198; Grote,
11, 332. — 8. **τοὺς μὲν**...**παραδοῦναι δέ**, *and handing it over to them,
thus wronging you his former allies.* So we may express in idiomatic
English the force of μὲν...δέ. — 10. **Μαγνησίαν**...**ὑποσχέσθαι.** Cf.
Phil. II. 24: **Μαγνησίαν ἐδίδου.** The dismission of the Olynthian
ambassadors took place B. C. 358 - 7; the capture and transfer of
Potidæa, 356; and the engagements in regard to Magnesia and the
Phocian War (often called the Second Sacred War), 353. The fulfil-
ment of the promise in regard to Magnesia did not take place till
after the close of that war, which lasted ten years, 356 - 46. — **ὅλως,**
in fine. — 14. **ἄνοιαν.** Dem. attributes εὐήθεια to his own coun-
trymen, but ἄνοια to foreigners. W. — **ἀεί,** *from time to time.* —
15. **προσλαμβάνων**, *taking advantage of.* See προσαγαγόμενον used
in essentially the same sense above, and observe the difference between the aor. part., which denotes a completed action, and the
imperf., which expresses a continued and repeated action. — **οὕτως,**
sc. by deceiving and taking advantage: emphatic resumption. —
8. 16. **διὰ τούτων**, *through the instrumentality of these persons*
(peoples). So Franke and Rehdantz. But editors generally: *by these*

arts. The language and the argument will admit of either. Dem. believed that Philip would be *pulled down* by the *very same persons* and *the very same means* by which he was *raised to greatness.* (Observe the exact antithesis between καθαιρεθῆναι and ἤρθη). But ἕκαστοι, which naturally refers to τούτων, and which *must* mean *persons,* is in favor of the former interpretation. — 20. **καιροῦ...πράγματα,** *to such a crisis, then, the affairs of Philip have come.* καιροῦ is gen. after τοῦτο. C. 416 ; Cu. 412 ; G. 168, N. 2 ; H. 559, c. — 21. **ἤ** = *or else.* — 22. **ὡς...λέγω,** *that these things which I say are not true.* — 25. **δεδουλωμένοι** here denotes political subjection, not literal subjugation. It is pronounced an exaggeration by Whiston and most of the commentators.

9. 22. **Καὶ μήν,** *And verily.* Whiston : And then indeed. — **μὲν ...ἡγεῖται...οἴεται δέ,** *while he believes...yet thinks.* ἡγεῖται implies reasons by which one is *led* to believe or admit, while οἴεται expresses a mere supposition. — P. 14, l. 2. **τὰ χωρία καὶ λιμένας,** the use of one art. for the two nouns links them more closely : *the fortresses and harbors.* — 3. **ὑπ'...συστῇ.** The passive sense leads to a passive construction : *when affairs* (powers) *are held together by good-will.* — 5. **καὶ συμπονεῖν...ἄνθρωποι,** *the men* (who are concerned) *are willing* (*both,* καί, unnecessary in English) *to toil together and to bear the calamities* (incident to the war) *and to persevere.* Schaefer and Voemel regard the force of σύν as extending to φέρειν = *bear together ;* but this is not necessary. — 8. **ἰσχύσῃ,** *has become powerful,* cf. 1, 13, ἠσθένησε, fell sick. — 9. **ἀνεχαίτισε,** as well as πταῖσμα, refers primarily to a horse throwing his rider. It is gnomic aorist : *overthrows and scatters the whole.* —10. 10. **οὐκ ἔστιν,** *it is not possible,* IT IS NOT POSSIBLE. Cf. 1. 19. — **ἀδικοῦντα,** *by injustice,* the part. denoting means, and the pres. part. a continual course of injustice. —12. **τὰ τοιαῦτα,** such power as Philip's, and acquired by such means. — **ἤνθησεν.** Cf. Madv. Synt. 111 a : "The aor. is used of that which has often happened and consequently (in single instances) is wont to happen, in which use it is sometimes connected with the present." The figure contained in ἤνθησεν is kept up through the sentence. The whole passage may be rendered thus : *such powers hold out* (cf. ἀντέχῃ, 1. 25) *in a single instance and for a short time and flourish exceedingly mayhap in the hopes* (which they excite), *but in and by the lapse of time their weakness is discovered, and they fall beneath their own weight.* τῷ χρόνῳ

denotes means. Cf. 1, 18. περὶ αὑτά, lit. *about themselves*, like
drooping flowers round the stem of the plant. — 16. **τὰ κάτωθεν,**
strictly the parts from below upwards, and particularly *the lower
parts.*

11. 22. ὅπως...οὕτως, that is, *the better and quicker the way any
one proposes the more I shall be pleased.* — 23. **πρὸς δέ,** δέ should be
rendered *and also,* to correspond with μέν. — **ταῦτα** is referred by
Schaefer and Franke to the weakness and instability of Philip's power,
as above described ; but better, with Rehdantz, Westermann, Whiston, Heslop, and others, to refer it to the purpose of sending aid.
Cf. 1, 2 : ταῦτ᾽ ερεῖ, where the same twofold counsel is given. —
26. **λογοὺς ποιεῖσθαι** = *to remonstrate.* Cf. 1, 22, note on κεκωλύκασι. — **12.** P. 15, line 3. **ἅπας μὲν λόγος,** *all words,* no matter
whose, *but especially* (μάλιστα δέ) those that come from (παρά) Athens.
τὰ πράγματα, *the* corresponding *actions.* — 6. **δοκοῦμεν** refers to the
common opinion or *reputation* (δόξα) of the Athenians in this respect,
viz. as excelling in speech. — **13. 8. μετάστασιν** is properly the
changed state resulting from μεταβολήν, which is the *act* or *process* of
change.   But Dem. uses the *pair* as usual for emphasis, which he
further enforces by repeating and varying the adjective : *much, then,
is the change and great the revolution you must show.* — 9. **εἰσφέροντας** agrees with ὑμᾶς implied in δεικτέον = δεικνύναι ὑμᾶς δεῖ. —
10. **κἂν ἐθελήσητε,** *if you are resolved* (aorist) *to carry these things
through to their consummation* (πέρας, Lat. per) *as it becomes and
behooves you to do.*

14. 16. "Ολως. *On the whole.* — **γάρ** introduces the proof of the
clause immediately preceding, viz. that his own kingdom and power
are in a bad state. — 17. **ἐν μὲν...μέρει,** *as an auxiliary,* lit. in the
role of an adjunct ; opposed to **αὑτὴ δέ,** *but itself by itself.*   Dem. was
the first of the Athenian statesmen to discover and expose the ambitious designs of Philip.   But *he* was slow to appreciate the new and
strange power which Macedon was to derive from the personal influence and military genius of this one man. — **οἶον,** *as, for instance, it
once joined you under Timotheus against the Olynthians.*   In 364 B. C.
the Athenians, under command of Timotheus, entered Thrace, and,
aided by Perdiccas, king of Macedon, made a successful campaign,
though they did not subdue the Olynthians. — 19. **πάλιν αὖ,** *again,
on the other hand, against Potidæa for the Olynthians, this force consisting of both together* (Macedonians and Olynthians) *proved to be*

something considerable. This was in B. C. 357. See Grote 11, 334.
πάλιν introduces a second instance, while αὖ marks the change of
sides, *for* Olynthus instead of *against* it. — **νυνί,** *quite recently.* —
21. **ἐπὶ...οἰκίαν,** *against the reigning family,* sc. the despots of
Pheræ, B. C. 352. — **πάντ'** is usually taken adverbially, *it helps altogether,* i. e. *essentially.* It can, however, be taken as subject of
ὠφελεῖ, *all helps,* like our proverb, every little helps. So Whiston,
and apparently Dindorf and Sauppe. — 15. 25. **οἷς** = *wherein.* —
26. **ἐπισφαλεστέραν,** sc. δύναμιν, *has rendered it still more insecure.*
— P. 16, l. 3. **τοῦτο ἐξήλωκε,** *and has made this his passion.* Whiston. The change of tense and of gender both intensify the expression. — 4. **ἂν...τι,** *whatever may happen.* — 4 – 6. **τὴν...δόξαν,** the
separation of the art. from the subs. is noticed by the commentators.
Heslop refers to Phil. II. 29, where twenty-nine words intervene
between the art. and its participle. — 5. **μηδείς** instead of οὐδείς, because it is subjective and represents Philip's view of the case. —
16. 7. **φιλοτιμίας,** see note, § 3. — **κοπτόμενοι,** *harassed,* lit. stricken,
Eng. chop. — **ἄνω κάτω.** The omission of the connection *represents*
the rapidity of Philip's movement, *up and down,* in which he resem-
bled Napoleon. — 9. **ταλαιπωροῦσιν,** *toil and suffer.* — 9 – 11. **οὔτ'**
...οὔτ'...οὔθ', *neither being allowed to employ themselves on their occupations nor on their private concerns, nor being able to dispose of such
things as they may perchance have earned in such ways as they can.*
The οὔτ'...οὔτ' together correlate with οὔθ'...ἔργοις, which refers especially, but not exclusively, to agricultural works. — 12. **κεκλειμένων,**
κ. τ. λ, gen. abs., giving the reason — *because* the markets are closed.
— 17. 16. **πεζέταιροι,** foot attendants, that is, *body guards.* — **δόξαν
μέν,** well rendered by Heslop, *have the reputation, it is true* (μέν), *of
being admirable soldiers and thoroughly trained in matters pertaining
to war.* — **συγκεκροτημένοι,** lit. welded together, see L. & S. — **ἐγώ,**
emphatic. — 18. **τῶν...γεγενημένων,** *who have been in the very country*
of Philip. — **ἤκουον,** *was hearing,* sc. recently. — 19. **οὐδένων,** *they
are no better than others.* — 20. **οἷος** is not entirely pleonastic = *of a
character experienced in war and campaigns.* — 21. **τούτους,** pl. referring to those implied in εἴ τίς = siquis, *whoever.* μέν resumptive of
μέν in the previous clause. — **φιλοτιμία** is here used more nearly in
its literal sense, love of honor, that is, *ambition,* or *jealousy.* — 24.
εἶναι, sc. ἔφη; so in § 19 again. — 25. **ἄλλως,** *otherwise* = *generally; temperate or upright generally,* sc. in other virtues besides tem-

perance. — **τὴν...μέθην.** These vices are attributed to Philip by more impartial witnesses than Demosthenes. Cf. Ath. 6. 260; Polyb. 8, 11, et al.; but, as Whiston remarks, they were so controlled as to help rather than hinder his success among his wild and half-civilized subjects and neighbors. On the character of Philip, see especially Thirlwall, II. p. 62, Amer. ed. — 27. **ἐν οὐδενὸς...μέρει,** *of no account. οὐδενός* is not neuter, as Heslop makes it. Cf. § 14, and L. & S. *μέρει* = class, roll = accounted *as* no one. — 19. P. 17, l. 1. **λοιποὺς δή,** *so then there are left about him brigands and flatterers.* According to Schaefer, *λῃστάς* is opposed to *σώφρων, κόλακας* to *δίκαιος.* — 2. **τοιούτους...οἵους,** men of such character as = *men who will get drunk and perform such dances,* the *κορδακισμούς* of the previous section. Heslop. — 5. **ἀπήλαυνον,** were accustomed to scout, *always scouted.* — 6. **Καλλίαν.** Nothing else is known of him. The Scholiast says, he was a domestic who was condemned, fled to Macedonia, and stopped with Philip. — 7. **ἐκεῖνον,** here in a bad sense, *that infamous Callias, the public slave.* — 8. **μίμους, κ. τ. λ.,** *actors of farces and makers of lewd songs.* In old English, as in Greek, poets were called "makers." — 20. 12. **γνώμης** is generic = sentiment, or *character, κακοδαιμονίας* is specific = ill-starred folly, *infatuation.* — 14. **κατορθοῦν** inf. with *αὐτόν* understood as subject = *his successful career* (inf. *pres.*). — **αἱ εὐπραξίαι.** The art. is generic = *success,* or *successes* in general : *successes are mighty to hide such scandals.* — 16. **πταίσει,** cf. *πταῖσμα,* § 9. — **τότ' ἀκριβῶς, κ. τ. λ.,** *then these* vices *of his will be fully exposed,* lit. closely scrutinized. — 17. **δείξει.ν.** The best authorities agree that this verb is impers. = *it will appear,* or the event will show, of which use Sauppe cites numerous examples. — **οὐκ εἰς μακράν,** *at no distant period.* — 18. **ἂν...βουλήσθε,** *if the gods will, and you so resolve.* So Whiston. And Hermann, Sauppe, and Dindorf recognize the same distinction. See note, I. 1. Demosthenes uses **θέλειν** (not *ἐθέλειν,* still less *βούλεσθαι*), of the gods. — 21. 19. **τέως,** though Ionic, is found here and elsewhere in Dem. in the best MSS. and editions. Cf. L. & S. II. — **πάντα κινεῖται,** *all* the members *are affected, whether it be a rupture or a sprain, or if any other part of the system be unsound.* Cf. De Cor. 198, where this favorite simile is repeated in a little different form. — 25. **συμπλακῇ,** lit. *may be grappled with.* Render : *whenever they may be entangled in a war on their borders, it makes all clearly manifest.* **πάντα** answers to *πάντα κινεῖται,* and has respect particularly to the

diseases of the body politic. ἔκδηλα is opposed to ἀφανῆ, and implies the bringing of these diseases *out* to the light of day. — ἐποίησεν, gnomic aorist.

22. P. 18, l. 2 – 5. σώφρονος μέν...οὐ μὴν ἀλλ', *he uses the reasoning of a wise man, I admit...nevertheless.* — 3. τὸ ὅλον, the whole,
that is, it is *every thing.* Compare De Cor. 194, where he says, Fortune
is mistress of all, κύριος τῶν πάντων. — παρά, *through the entire course
of.* — 6. τύχην, cf. note, I. 1. — 8. ἀφορμάς, lit. starting points,
here *grounds*, or *reasons: far more grounds for obtaining the good-will
of the gods.* — 23. 10. οἶμαι, *methinks.* — 11. αὐτόν, *while he is doing nothing himself.* — 12. μή τί γε, much less. Cf. 717. — 14. αὐτός, *in person.* — 17. οὐδέ...ἐγώ, *and I do not wonder at this.* —
24. 20. εἰ = *that.* — 21 – 25. μέν ποτε...νυνὶ δέ, *although once...yet
now.* — Λακ...ἀντήρατε, *you withstood the Lacedæmonians,* sc. in the
Bœotian war, B. C. 378. — 23. ὑμῖν ἐξόν, *when it was in your power.*
— οἱ ἄλλοι, *the other* Greeks = all the others. — 24. ἀνηλίσκετε.
Observe the change from the aor. to the imperf.: *were continually
spending.* — 27. τοὺς μὲν ἄλλους, *after often saving the rest of the
Greeks collectively and every one of them individually in turn, you
nevertheless sit still when you have lost your own,* i. e. Amphipolis,
Pydna, Methone, and Potidæa. W. — καθ' is distributive, *one by
one.* — P. 19, l. 5. πολεμεῖτε, *you have been and still are carrying on
the war,* sc. ten years, reckoning from the capture of Amphipolis. —
6. τί ποιούντων, *what you have been doing while all this* (οὗτος is
emphatic) *has passed away,* lit. *while you have been doing what, all
this,* etc. — ἔστε γὰρ δήπου, *for you know surely.* — 7. αὐτῶν is opposed to ἑτέρους, *procrastinating yourselves, hoping that somebody else
would act.* — 9. κρινόντων, *bringing one another to trial.* This spirited passage is made more lively and rapid by the omission of the
connectives. — 26. 10. εἶθ'...γενήσεσθαι, *are you then so senseless as
to cherish the hope that the affairs of the state will become prosperous
instead of bad by the very same measures by which they have become
bad instead of prosperous.* The irresistible logic of this passage is
further enforced by the careful antithesis of the words and the rhetorical order of the two clauses. — 15. πολὺ γάρ, *for in the nature of
things it is in all cases much easier to keep what you have than to get
what you have not.* The commentators differ widely as to the construction of the words, some connecting πολὺ ῥᾷον adverbially with
φυλάττειν, and making πάντα the subject of πέφυκεν, and others mak-

ing πολὺ ῥᾷον pred. after πέφυκεν and πάντα obj. of κτήσασθαι (πάντα, lit. all things, i. e. anything = *in all cases*). I have followed the latter. In Ol. I. 23, the orator seems to express just the opposite sentiment. But there he is speaking of the intoxicating influence of prosperity ; here only of what would otherwise be true in the *nature of the case :* hence, there he says it *oftentimes seems* more difficult to keep than to get ; here, *in the nature of things*, it is much easier to keep anything than to get it. Prudentibus quidem facilius est, sed imprudentibus difficilius. Dind. — 17. ὅ τι...οὐδέν, *nothing whatever.* — 19. αὐτῶν...ἤδη, *this, therefore, is our own duty already.* ἤδη is emphatic = *and that immediately.* Cf. Phil. 1. 8 : ἦν ἀποθέσθαι φημὶ δεῖν ἤδη. — 27. 21. πρὶν...κρατήσητε, *before you shall have become masters of the position.* So Whiston. Heslop renders τῶν πραγμάτων *your objects*, sc. the deliverance of Olynthus. — 22. ἀπ᾽ αὐτῶν τῶν ἔργων, *from the acts themselves*, not from the rumors and reports of them. — 23. τὰς προφάσεις, *to remove the excuses* (of the generals) *and the defaults on your own part* (which furnished the pretext for those excuses). — P. 20, l. 2, 3. φεύγειν... εὑρίσκειν. The Scholiast remarks that the orator is hinting especially at Chares. — 4. ἐνταῦθα, *here*, i. e. in the wars to which they were sent by the Athenians ; so ἐκεῖ below, *there*, sc. in their own private wars. — 5. Ἀμφίπολις Dindorf would change to Ἀμφίπολιν, as the obj. of κομεῖσθε, and Franke, Rehdantz, Voemel, Westermann, and others agree with him and with the MSS. in omitting αὐτήν after παραχρῆμα. — 6. οἱ δὲ κίνδυνοι, κ. τ. λ., *and the dangers belong exclusively to the officers, and pay there is none.* — 8. λήμματα, *gains*, lit. gettings, or takings ; generally used in a bad sense. ἆθλα = prizes of honorable war ; λήμματα = the gains of piracy and freebooting. See Schaefer in loc. — 9. Lampsacus and Sigeum, cities on the Asiatic side of the Hellespont, the latter near the Ægean and the former near the mouth of the Propontis, were given to Chares by the Persian satrap Artabanus for some service rendered him. On the Athenian armaments at this time, see Grote, XI. 312, and the authorities cited in his notes. — 29. 12. ἀποβλέψητε, *look away, look only.* — 13. δόντες λόγον, *having given them the opportunity to speak for themselves*, or, as we say, having given them a hearing. — 17. πρότερον μέν, κ. τ. λ., *for formerly, gentlemen of Athens, you used to make your extraordinary contributions by classes, but now you administer the government by classes ; an orator is at the head of either party, and a general under him, and the men to shout, three hundred;* al. οἱ τριακόσιοι, *the* three hundred. 1200 of the richest citizens of Athens (120 from each tribe) were selected whose duty it was to bear the heaviest burdens of taxation, and especially to advance money on any emergency, with the right, however, to reimburse themselves in part by collections from other citizens. These were divided into four classes (συμμορίαι), according to their property, 300 in each class, each class having a ἡγεμών, or chairman, at its head. These facts are sufficient to make the satire or burlesque in the text intelligible. For further details, which, however, are obscure and uncertain, see Dic. of Antiq. under εἰσφορά. Scholars have perplexed themselves needlessly by seeking too close an analogy between the symmorial and the political parties. Demosthenes was himself head of a symmoria for ten years. Or. con. Meidias, § 200. See also Or. περὶ Συμμορίων. — 21. προσνενέμησθε, *attach yourselves,* or *are attached.* — ὡς = *to,* see Lex. and Gram. — 30. 22. ὑμῶν...γενομένους, *and having become now also still* (as formerly) *your own masters* (instead of letting your political and party leaders be your lords and masters). — κοινόν, *alike free to all.* — 25 – 27. τοῖς μὲν...τοῖς δὲ...τοῖς δέ, sc. the politicians...the wealthy and industrious citizens...and the mass of voters. — 25. ἀποδώσετε, tanquam debitum (Franke), not merely *give,* but *give up* or *give over.* — ὑμῶν limits τυραννίδος, and is objective genitive (cf. Or. de Cor. 66 : τυραννίδα τῶν Ἑλλήνων) = *to give orders as if from a despotic government over you.* — 26. τριηραρχεῖν...στρατεύεσθαι. Heslop, Rehdantz, Funkhaenel, and some other editors omit the commas between these infinitives, as all the editions and the orator himself omit the connectives to emphasize the rapid list of services required of this class. — P. 21, l. 4. περιέσται, *it will remain.* Some of the best editors follow S, and read ἔξεσται, *you will have the opportunity.* — 31. κεφάλαιον, *I recommend, then, in sum that all.* Heslop. Observe the emphatic recurrence three times over of this ALL, by which popular catchword the orator skilfully recommends the true democracy of equal burdens and services. — 5. τὸ ἴσον, *that which is just and equal,* that is, according to his property, as the preceding clause defines it. — 6. κατὰ μέρος, *in turn,* that is, *in rotation.* The same thing is expressed (Phil. I. 21) by ἐκ διαδοχῆς, *in succession.* — 7. λόγον διδόναι, cf. note on δόντες λόγον, § 29. Render : *to give a hearing* (continuously or successively is implied in the pres. inf.) *to all who come forward*, sc. to speak from the bema. — 8. ὁ δεῖνα indefinitely expresses a definite person.   C. 245.   The orator is supposed to have meant Eubulus and his friends. — 9. τὸν εἰπόντα, the speaker, sc. Demosthenes.   The orator concludes very simply with a concise *resumé* of his main points, and leaves as the last impression on the minds of his hearers the pleasant thought of the self-approval and the advantage to the state which will result from the adoption of the measures that he recommends.

ΟΛΥΝΘΙΑΚΟΣ Γ.

1. Page 22, line 1. **Οὐχὶ ταὐτά,** not at all the same, that is, *very different are the thoughts which are suggested to me.* ταὐτά is grammatically the object of γιγνώσκειν, which Demosthenes is fond of using to express a thought or sentiment. — 2. **ἀποβλέψω,** *look away,* sc. *from* the bema and the speeches made there, and *into* the real state of public affairs. Cf. ἀποβλέψητε, Ol. II. § 29. — 3. **πρὸς τοὺς λόγους** would strictly require a somewhat different verb, e. g. βλέψω. The introduction of Cato's speech, as preserved in Sal. Cat., 52, 2, is a manifest imitation of this. — 5. **εἰς τοῦτο...ὥστε,** *have come into such a state that.* — **δέον** is explained by Madvig, Klotz, and the majority of commentators as depending on ὁρῶ by a peculiar species of attraction. The sense, however, is the same as if it were δέον εἶναι or ἐστί. — 9. **οὐχὶ τὴν οὖσαν,** *not at all the real* subject before you, which was the succor of Olynthus. — **ἁμαρτάνειν** is limited by **οὐδὲν ἄλλο** (acc. of respect or adv. acc.) in the first part of the sentence, and by the participle in the second = *to err simply in presenting.* — 12. **καὶ μάλα ἀκριβῶς,** *perfectly well,* καί intensive. — **ἐπ' ἐμοῦ,** *in my own time.* — 14. **τὴν πρώτην,** *as the first step.* Heslop. This emphasizes the idea already implied in προλαβεῖν, *to provide.* — 15. **ἐὰν γάρ,** well rendered by Heslop : *when this has been effectively secured, we may then go on* (καί) *to consider the question how we* (lit. *some one,* quite expressive of the comparative *indefiniteness* and *remoteness* of this work) *are to punish him ; but before we have laid the foundation rightly* (Ol. II. 10, τὰς ἀρχὰς καὶ τὰς ὑποθέσεις) *I consider it idle to say anything whatever about the end.* — **τοῦ,** of course, agrees with the entire clause τίνα...ἐκεῖνον. This exordium is more abrupt, direct, and earnest than than that of either of the preceding orations, and seems to imply a more pressing emergency in public affairs. Its object is to correct at once a fatal mistake in the drift of the foregoing discussion.

3. 22. **ἐγὼ δ' οὐκ,** *and yet I do not think it the most difficult question what advice ought to be given touching the present state of your affairs, but this is the difficulty which perplexes me.* **ἐκεῖνο** magnifies the difficulty and perplexity.—P. 23, l. 3. **παρὼν καὶ ἀκούων,** *by personal knowledge and by hearsay.* — 4. **σύνοιδα,** sc. *ὑμῖν = as you also do.* So Franke and Rehdantz, although the word does not necessarily mean anything more than *full* knowledge. — **τὰ πλείω** is followed by **ἢ** as if the article were omitted ; lit. *the more of your advantages have slipped out of your hands by your unwillingness to do your duty than by your not understanding them.* **τὰ πλείω** usually means the greater *part,* the most. The Or. here compliments the intelligence of the Athenians at the expense of their patriotism, or, rather, their will and purpose (**βούλεσθαι**). See notes on Ol. II. 23, and I. 1. **μὴ βούλεσθαι** denotes want of resolution rather than want of disposition. — 6. **ἀξιῶ δέ,** *and I request you, if I address you with frankness, to bear with me, considering this whether I speak the truth and* (speak it) *for this purpose that the future may become better.* — **διά** here = *for* as in modern Greek. — 9. **πρὸς χάριν,** *for popular favor, popularity.* — 10. **πᾶν μοχθηρίας,** *complete demoralization.*

4. 11. **μικρά** is used adverbially = *briefly,* and **γεγενημένων** is gen. after **ὑπομνῆσαι.** So Westermann, Franke, Rehdantz, etc. Others (e. g. Schaefer, Dindorf, Heslop) make **μικρά** = **ὀλίγα,** *a few,* and obj. of **ὑπομνῆσαι,** which can govern either two acc. or an acc. and gen. — 13. **ὅτ' ἀπηγγέλθη,** *when* Philip was reported, etc., i. e. you remember not merely the fact (**ὅτι**), but the time and the circumstances, which he proceeds to describe. — 14. **τρίτον...τουτί,** *now three or four years ago.* C. 482, c ; Cu. 405, Obs. 1 ; G. 161, N. ; H. 550 c. The time was more than three years, and less than four. See, however, Grote XI. 469, note, for a different view. — **'Ηραῖον Τεῖχος** was a fortress in Thrace near the Chersonese. It is identified by most commentators with a fortress of the same name near Perinthus ; but this is doubtful. See Grote, XI. 428. — **τότε τοίνυν,** well expressed by Heslop : *well it was then.* — **μαιμακτηριών,** November. — **πολλῶν δέ, κ. τ. λ.,** not *after* (Kennedy), which would require **γενομένου,** but *in the midst of much discussion and tumult,* that is, while it was going on, **γιγνομένου.** For the numb. of this part., see C. 497 ; H. 511 h ; G. 138, N. 2. — 16. **παρ' ὑμῖν,** in your presence, that is, *in your assembly.* — 18. **μέχρι,** *up to,* more expressive of the exigency than *under.* This levy included all the citizens who were liable to military service beyond the bounds of Attica. — 19. **εἰσφέρειν,** *to raise a war-tax.* See Dic. Ant. **εἰσφορά.** — 20. **διελθόντος...ἐνιαυτοῦ,** *this year having passed away,* i. e. the

remaining seven months of it. The Attic year began with Heca-tombeon, i. e. in July. Add the three months of the next year named by the orator, and ten months elapse between the resolution and its execution or rather abortion. He draws out the *picture* of delay and final failure in sarcastic detail, counting them, as it were, on his fingers. It is hardly necessary to supply a verb in English. 21. **τούτου...μόγις,** *in the course of this last-named month, hardly.* — 22. **μετὰ τὰ μυστήρια.** For these must of course be celebrated ! The sarcasm still continues. The Mysteries were celebrated during nine days, from the 15th to the 23d of Boëdromion. For the time of the Attic months, and the significance of the names, see Lex. and Dic. Ant. — **δέκα...ἀργυρίου.** The failure, too, is drawn out in detail : *ten* ships instead of *forty* — *empty,* i. e. unmanned, in contrast with the levy of citizens *in mass* — and with *five* talents instead of *sixty.* Charidemus was left to man the ships with mercenaries. Charidemus was a native of Oreus in Bœotia, an adopted citizen of Athens, and a commander of mercenary troops, especially in the Chersonese. See Dic. of Biog. — 25. **ἀμφότερα,** both reports. — **ἦλθε,** raro usu de nun-tiis. Schaefer. — 27. **ἦν...αὐτός,** *but this* was *the very opportunity,* sc. when Philip was sick or dead. — P. 24, l. 2. **ἠνώχλει.** Observe the force of the imp.: *would not have been preserved to be troubling us as he now is.*

6. 3. **οὐκ...ἔχοι,** *cannot be altered,* strictly could not if we would. — 4. **ἑτέρου,** sc. the Olynthiac. — **τις** = *a sort of,* not so good as that we lost, but one of some considerable value. — **δι' ὅν,** *by reason of which,* really, for the sake of which. — 5. **τί...τούτῳ.** C. 478 ; Cu. 401 ; Madv. 27. R. 1. — 7. **θεάσασθε,** *behold how* you *will have conducted the whole war in behalf of Philip,* sc. as if you had been his generals. — 7. 9. **ὑπῆρχον.** The series of clauses without connec-tives, extending through the section, explain the **θεάσασθε ὃν τρόπον** by a rapid, distinct, and vivid enumeration of particulars descriptive of the status at the beginning of the war : *there were, to begin with, the Olynthians possessed of some power.* — 11. **οὔτε...ἐθάρρει,** *neither Philip felt secure in regard to them, nor they in regard to Philip.* **θαρρεῖν τινι** = to rely upon one, but **θαρρεῖν τινα** = to feel secure (without anxiety) in regard to any one. — 12. **ἐπράξαμεν...εἰρήνην,** *we negotiated peace* (with them) *and they with us.* It seems necessary to supply **πρὸς ἐκείνους,** although Schaefer (followed apparently by Whiston) makes **πρὸς ἡμᾶς** = **πρὸς ἀλλήλους,** which would certainly

require πρὸς ἡμᾶς αὐτούς. The peculiar form seems to be chosen to express the *mutual* readiness of the parties for peace. — 13. ὥσπερ... δυσχερές, *an obstruction, as it were, and an offence.* — 14. ἐφορμεῖν, lit. to lie at anchor, hence *to be on the watch for.* This clause explains τοῦτο. — τοῖς ἑαυτοῦ καιροῖς, *the opportunities which he gave.* —15. ἐκπολεμῶσαι. See note Ol. I. 7, where we have the same thing in nearly the same words. — 17. ὁπωσδήποτε, *somehow or other*, the orator does not say how, but implies (what he *says* in Ol. I. 7, γέγονεν αὐτόματον) that it was without the agency of the Athenians. — 8. τί οὖν introduces the conclusion from the series of clauses without connectives in the foregoing section. — 19. ἐγὼ μέν. μέν solitarium, as the old grammarians called it, i. e. without a corresponding δέ expressed. It implies a counter-conception in the mind of the speaker, which *he* cannot entertain, however others may think. — χωρὶς γάρ, κ. τ. λ., *for aside from the disgrace which would encompass us.* The inf. and part. take ἄν, when it would belong to the finite verbs, of which they take the place. C. 618; Cu. 595; G. 211; H. 803. — 21. οὐδέ = καὶ οὐ, *I see that there is also no small reason to fear the consequences.* — 22. ἐχόντων...ἡμῖν, *the Thebans being affected towards us as they are*, sc. unkindly; euphemism. As Heslop remarks, the feeling was fully reciprocated. Cf. De Cor. 18. — χρήμασιν, *in their resources*, sc. those derived from the plunder of the temple at Delphi. They had coined 10,000 talents ($10,000,000 in round numbers) from the consecrated vases and statues alone. — 24. μηδενός implies a supposition = *in case there was no one to prevent him after having subjected what he now has in hand* (Olynthus) *from turning his attention to things here* (in Athens). The reader will observe the euphemisms. — 9. 26. εἰς τοῦτο, *to this extent* = *till then.* The procrastination is emphasized by the use of the *future* inf. (ποιήσειν) instead of the pres. or aor. C. 660; H. 718; Madv. 171, R. 2: *is putting off his going to do his duty.* — P. 25, l. 3. εἰς τοῦτο, *to this result.* Observe the emphatic position : *for that this is the result to which matters will come if we throw away our present advantages we are pretty well aware all of us, of course.*

10. 9. παράδοξον. He conciliates his hearers by this admission at the outset, that his proposal is contrary to their opinions and inclinations. — 10. καθίσατε, *appoint* (lit. cause to sit) *law-makers*; al. καθίστατε; but καθίσατε is the *regular* word, and the aorist tense seems to be required here. Special nomothetæ are here intended, for

the special purpose of abrogating the existing theoric law. The ordinary nomothetæ were drawn by lot at the beginning of the year from the heliastæ. See Dic. Antiq. Νομοθέτης. — ἐν δὲ τούτοις, *and in the session of these law-makers.* — 11. 13. θεωρικῶν. In reference to this fund, which was originally set apart for the maintenance of the religious festivals ("church-fund," Grote), but was extended to provide tickets of admission to the theatre, etc., see Dic. Antiq. s. v.; Grote, XI. 491. The views of Demosthenes, in regard to appropriating this fund to war purposes, which he insinuates in each of his Olynthiacs, and urges more directly and earnestly in the third, were realized just before the battle of Chæronea, when it was too late, — twelve years after he had begun to enforce them. — σαφῶς οὑτωσί, *thus explicitly.* The Athenians at this time were so passionately fond of their theatres, spectacles, and shows, that they had made it a penal offence (a *capital* offence, according to Ulpian, questioned, however, by Grote) even to move the diversion of the theoric fund to military uses. Demosthenes, it will be seen, does not make such a motion directly ; he only moves the appointment of a legislative committee for the purpose. — 14. ἐνίους, *some of them.* — οἱ μέν, *the former,* sc. the laws about the theoric fund : οἱ δέ, *the latter,* sc. those about military service. — 15. θεωρικά, *as show-money.* — οἱ δέ, κ. τ. λ., *while the latter shield from punishment those who shirk military service,* lit. those who do not take their place in the ranks, probably on various pretexts furnished by the laws, not merely those classes who were expressly exempted from service. — 16. εἶτα καί, *and thus also.* — 18. ἐπειδὰν δέ, κ. τ. λ., *and when you have abrogated these things* (meaning the laws, but using a more sweeping expression), *and have made it safe* (lit. the way safe) *to say what is for your highest good, then and not till then,* etc. — 12. 21. μὴ σκοπεῖτε, *do not be looking to see who for having said what is best* FOR *you will take measures to be destroyed* BY *you.* Observe the juxtaposition of ὑπὲρ ὑμῶν ὑφ᾿ ὑμῶν, in which the likeness of sound adds emphasis to the opposition in sense. — 23. ἄλλως τε καί, *especially* (see explanations in Lex. and Gr.) *when this is going to be the only result,* viz. *that the adviser and mover of these measures should suffer wrongfully some harm.* — P. 26, l. 1. καὶ λύειν γε, *yes, and you ought to require that the very same persons* (Eubulus and his party) *take measures* (inf. pres.) *to abrogate the laws who have been the authors of them.* — 13. 3. οὐ γάρ ἐστι, κ. τ. λ., *for it is not right that the then authors of the laws should continue to enjoy the popularity* (of a law) *which has injured the whole state, while the odium* (of legislation) *whereby we should all be benefited should damage him who has now given you the best advice.* The reader cannot fail to notice the nice adjustment of antithetic words and phrases even to the πᾶσαν and ἄπαντες, and the τότε and νῦν. — 7. μηδαμῶς...ὑμῖν, *do not by any means expect any man to be so powerful with you.*

14. 12. Οὐ μὴν οὐδ'. *Nay, more, you ought not to be ignorant of this, surely.* The statement is self-evident, and yet of vital moment ; hence the emphatic combination of particles. — 13 - 15. ἄν μὴ...ὑμᾶς, *unless there be superadded the willingness to execute at least what you have resolved, heartily yourselves.* ὑμᾶς is emphatic ; also ποιεῖν. — 16. ἤ...διαπράξασθαι, *or to accomplish the objects for which they may have been proposed.* γραφῇ is 2 aor. subj. pass. with ψηφίσματα for its subject. — 18. μικρά, *few.* — ἐπράττετε, *be performing,* distinctly bringing the action or rather inaction down to the present time : ὑβρίκει, *have insulted,* without any allusion to the present. ἄν influences both these verbs. — 20. ἕνεκα retains here essentially its original sense, *on account of :* so far as RESOLUTIONS *at least* could have *effected* the *result,* or, so far as it *depended* on RESOLUTIONS *at any rate.* — **15.** 21. τὸ γὰρ πράττειν, *for doing while it is posterior to speaking and voting in order of time is prior and superior to them in efficiency.* — 24. τὰ δ' ἄλλα, *and the others you have,* to wit, the speaking and voting, as explained in the following clause, viz. orators to give you the necessary advice, and of all men the quickest discernment to judge of what they say. A delicate compliment to season the sarcasm which precedes. — 26. καὶ πρᾶξαι δέ, *yes, and you will be able to* DO *also now, if you act with proper efficiency,* or, perhaps, as Westermann explains, *if you begin it right,* lit. MAKE *it right.* πράττειν is to *do, practice, perform ;* ποιεῖν *to make, effect,* or *create.* Phil. I. 11 : you will soon *create* (ποιήσετε) another Philip ; Phil. III. 52 : and they *create* (ποιοῦσιν) for him leisure to *do* (πράττειν) whatever he pleases. πράττειν is here opposed to λέγειν and χειροτονεῖν, and πρᾶξαι to εἰπεῖν and γνῶναι, as *doing* is to *speaking* and *voting,* and distinguished from ποιεῖν as *doing* from *making* an opportunity. The distinction between πράττειν and ποιεῖν is not always carefully observed. — **16.** P. 27, l. 4. ἄνθρωπος, Philip. Observe the emphasis on ἄνθρωπος and ἄπαντα in the reversal of the logical order of subject and object. — ταύτης, Olynthus and the Chalcidic peninsula. — 5. πάν-

τῶν, *of all men* (not of all things). — 5–7. **οὐχ...πολεμοῦνται**, *are not they whom we promised promptly to protect if they would engage in war* (with Philip), *are not these now actually engaged in war*, i. e. involved in war *by* Philip? The turn is spirited and elegant. Al. **πολεμοῦσιν**; but the reading rests on slight authority. — **σώσειν** instead of **βοηθήσειν**, Atheniensium gratia, paullo magnificentius loquitur. Franke. — 8. **βάρβαρος.** This is hardly just or fair ; for, although the Macedonians were a mixed race, and not pure Greek, their kings were usually recognized as descendants of the Grecian Hercules. Herod. 8, 137 ; Isoc. 5, 32 ; Thirl. II. 58. — **οὐχ...τις**, *is he not anything* (however base) *that any one might choose to call him?* This rapid fire of interrogations is characteristic and quite terrible. — 17. 9. **πάντα ἐάσαντες**, *having let them all go*, referring to **ἔχων τὰ ἡμέτερα.** — **μόνον οὐχί**, only not, i. e. *almost.* — 12. **ἐγώ** is doubly emphatic, **I** *know certainly.* — 16. **δήπου** is emphatic and satirical : *no doubt, of course.* Cf. § 9. — 17. **εἰ...ἐνίκων ἄν**, *and if each of them had done this, they would have been victorious.* The imperfect properly denotes the action as *continued*, begun in the past and continued to the present time = *if each of them were* (i. e. had been) *doing this* (continually), *they would be victorious.* But we express such conditions and conclusions less definitely in English. C. 631, b ; Cu. 543 ; G. 220, a, 2 ; H. 746. Cf. note De Cor. 9. — 18. 18. **καὶ νῦν**, *so also now*, that is, let every man act in civil affairs on the principle just illustrated by military ; let him do his own duty instead of finding fault with others, and Athens will triumph. — **οὐ λέγει τις**, *some one* (we will suppose) *does not give the best advice ; let another rise and speak and not be finding fault* (*pres.* imp.) *with him.* The two clauses are equivalent to the protasis and apodosis of a conditional sentence ; but they are put in a more lively and rhetorical form. So with the following clauses. Bekker and Dindorf make the first clause in each pair interrogative. But most editors give them as above. — 20. **ἀγαθῇ τύχῃ**, *do it and prosper*, lit. with good fortune. — 21. **οὐκέτι**, *no longer*, i. e. he is not responsible for not giving *agreeable* advice, as he would be on the previous supposition, viz. of not giving *good* advice. — 22. **πλὴν εἰ**, *unless when he ought to pray he fails to do so ; for to pray, gentlemen of Athens, is an easy matter, gathering together all his wishes in a small compass.* Orator ridet Athenienses qui omnia *εὐχαῖς* perfici posse sperarent. Schaefer. — 19. P. 28, l. 1. **πόρους ἑτέρους στρατιωτικούς**, *another* (i. e. a different) *way of raising money for the*

E

army. ἕτερος with its comparative termination is always one of two; if plural, one of two groups or classes. Heslop compares Ol. I. 20 : λέγουσι δὲ καὶ ἄλλους τινὰς ἄλλοι πόρους, and says : there his proposition is counted in as one of several ways suggested for meeting the difficulty ; here ἕτεροι πόροι stand collectively on the one side, and the theoric fund on the other. — 2. εἴποι τις ἄν, *some one may ask.* — 3. φήμ'...ἐστιν, *yes, indeed, if there is any such man.* So Westermann and Rehdantz, and this corresponds with the εἴ τις which precedes and the εἴ τῳ which follows. Others render, *if it is possible.* — 4. ἀλλὰ θαυμάζω, κ. τ. λ., *but I wonder if it ever has happened or ever will happen to any human being when he has spent what he has for useless objects to find in what he has not abundant means for necessary purposes.* The conciseness and point of the original are imperfectly expressed in any translation. — 7. μέγα...λόγοις, *is a great help to such arguments.* Kennedy. *Powerfully seconds.* Heslop. — 8. διόπερ, *and for this very reason.* — 10. τὰ δὲ πράγματα, κ. τ. λ., *but the facts are often in reality very different.* πέφυκεν, are in their nature, are in reality. Such gnomes, full of common sense and obvious almost as axioms, yet laying bare the human heart, and illustrating history, often illuminate the pages of Démosthenes. — 20. 11. ὁρᾶτε, κ. τ. λ., *look at these things therefore in such light as the facts also* (and not your wishes merely) *allow, and then you will be able to serve and have pay.* Whiston extends the influence of ὅπως over the whole sentence, and renders, *and so that you will be able,* and Heslop places no comma after ἐνδέχεται. — 14. ἐλλείποντας...φέρειν, *failing for want of money in any of the duties required by the war, to bear tamely such reproaches,* sc. as are incurred by such conduct. — 16. οὐδ' ἐπὶ μέν, κ. τ. λ., *no, nor after having seized arms and marched against Corinthians and Megarians to allow Philip to enslave Grecian cities for want of supplies for the soldiers.* The point of the passage lies in the *un-Hellenic* course which they pursued in resisting the petty warfare of Corinthians and Megarians (who were Greeks) upon one another or upon other Greeks, and allowing *Philip* (whom he stigmatizes as a barbarian) to *enslave* Grecian cities. "It is impossible to say with certainty to what events Demosthenes here alludes, nor need we conclude that his contemporaries were engaged in them." Whiston. It is generally supposed that he refers to events which occurred in the previous century, viz. the famous invasion of Megara by the Corinthians, B. C. 458, and the revolt of the Megarians and a consequent invasion of Megaris by the Athenians some fifteen years later.

21. 20. ταῦτ' is the object of **λέγειν**, *I have not said these things* (sc. about the theoric fund) *with the idle purpose of making some of you my enemies.* — **τὴν ἄλλως,** sc. **ὁδόν,** in the way that is otherwise than suitable or proper. See Lex. — **22. ἀτυχής,** *ill-starred.* — **24. τῶν πραγμάτων,** *the state.* — **25. χάριτος,** *popular favor,* as in § 13 above. — **25. καὶ γὰρ…πάνυ,** *for I hear, as probably you also do* (that is, it is commonly said, and we often hear it), *that the speakers in the times of our ancestors, whom your present advisers all praise but do not at all imitate.* — P. 29, l. 2. **τῆς πολιτείας,** *in their administration.* — **τὸν Ἀριστείδην,** C. 522 g ; Cu. 371 ; H. 530, a. — **ἐκεῖνος,** C. 542, b ; H. 679, b. Compare the Latin *ille.* — **3. τὸν… ἐμαυτῷ,** *my own namesake,* i. e. the Athenian general, who took Pylus from the Spartans in the Peloponnesian war. — **22. 4. οὗτοι** is disparaging and contemptuous, and opposed to **ἐκεῖνος,** as *iste* to *ille : but since these orators have made their appearance who are continually asking you, What is your pleasure ? what shall I move ? how can I oblige you ? the interests of the state have been recklessly bartered away for the popularity of the present moment.* — **χάριτος** is gen. of price. — **προπέποται** is well explained in the Lexicon. So we speak of *selling for a drink or a song.* — **7. τοιαυτί,** *such as you see.* — **23. 10. κεφάλαια,** here = *chief points of contrast.* — **12. γνώριμος,** *well known, familiar,* as shown in the explanatory clause **οὐ γὰρ ἀλλοτρίοις :** *for by using examples drawn, not from foreign lands, but in your own country, it is in your power to become prosperous.* — **24. 15. ἐκεῖνοι τοίνυν,** *well then, your ancestors, whom the speakers did not flatter nor caress, as these men now caress you.* **αὐτούς** follows **ἐφίλουν,** because it requires its object to be in the acc., while **ἐχαρίζονθ'** takes the dative. — **16. πέντε…ἔτη,** from B. C. 478 (when the maritime allies, renouncing the leadership of Sparta, ranged themselves under that of Athens) till the Peloponnesian war. — **17. ἑκόντων,** *with their consent.* This was the distinctive feature of that period of Athenian hegemony. By adding the twenty-eight years of the Peloponnesian war, Demosthenes, in his third Philippic, § 24, makes the whole duration of Athenian supremacy seventy-three years ; but the subjection in this latter period was *involuntary.* — **18. πλείω…τάλαντα.** Thucydides (2, 13) reckons the maximum at 9700 talents. The uncoined treasures of the Parthenon would make up the more

than 10,000. It is an immense sum for a small state = more than
$10,000,000 in gold, and in value ten times that sum. Cf. Böckh.,
Pub. Econ. 591. — εἰς...ἀνήγαγον, *brought up into the Acropolis*, sc.
into the Opisthodomus, where the public moneys were kept under the
guardianship of Athena. — 19. ὑπήκουε, *submitted to them;* hardly
true, certainly exaggerated. Perdiccas II., the king who was then
on the throne of Macedon (ὁ...ἔχων), was often at variance with the
Athenians, and always glad to make up with them ; in this sense
only did he submit to them. Observe the juxtaposition of αὐτοῖς and
βασιλεύς in emphatic contrast, a *king* to *them*, the Athenian *people*.
— 22. αὐτοὶ στρατευόμενοι, *serving in person*, and not relying on
mere mercenaries, — the point so often insisted on as the pivot of
the whole Olynthiac question. — 25. 27. οἰκοδομήματα, *edifices*, such
as the Propylæa, porticos, dock-yards, Piræus, etc. — κάλλη...ἱερῶν,
ornaments...of temples = *beautiful temples*, such as the Theseum,
Erechtheum, Parthenon, etc. — 26. P. 30, l. 3. ἰδίᾳ δέ, κ. τ. λ.,
while as individuals (in their private life) *they were so modest and so
exceedingly steadfast in abiding by the spirit of the constitution*, sc.
of the democracy. — 6. εἰ...ἐστίν, *if perchance any one of you knows
at all what kind of a house it is.* εἰ ἄρα = si forte, *if now, if perchance.* ἄρα and ποτέ both add to the severity of the implication that
it is very doubtful whether any of them know anything whatever about
the great men of previous generations. — 8. εἰς περιουσίαν, *for personal advantage*, opposed to τὸ κοινόν. — 12. ἴσως, *fairly, impar-
tially.* — εἰκότως, *naturally*, that is, as might have been expected. —
27. 13. τότε...προστάταις, *such now was the state of things with them
at that time enjoying the leaders of whom I have spoken.* — 15. ὑπὸ...
νῦν, *under the worthies of the present day.* —χρηστῶν, *excellent men!*
is of course ironical. The reference is to the popular orators, who
were the leading statesmen or politicians of the day. — 16. ἆρα...
παραπλησίως, *are they in a way* (or state) *at all similar, or even
resembling* that ? — 17. τὰ μέν...εἰπεῖν, *as to the rest I am silent,
though I could say much.* The MSS. generally and the majority
of the editions have οἷς before τὰ μέν ; and as the more difficult
reading it is entitled to the preference. But Schaefer and Sauppe
explain the οἷς as a repetition by some copyist of the last syllable of
the παραπλησίως which precedes ; and there is no suitable reference
or construction for it, — none on which commentators can at all
agree, and none which is consistent with the simplicity, the gram-

matical regularity, and the clearness which belong to Demosthenes. — 18. ἀλλ' is opposed to τὰ μὲν ἄλλα, *I pass over everything else, but I must speak of these.* — ὅσης, κ. τ. λ., *though favored with an absence of competitors so complete as you all see* (explained in the following specifications), *though the Lacedæmonians were ruined* (by the battle of Leuctra and the loss of their prowess in the Peloponnese), *and the Thebans were fully occupied* (by the Phocian war), *and of the rest no one was competent to contest the supremacy with us.* So the passage is well rendered by Heslop. — 22. ἐξὸν δέ, *and when it was in our power.* These clauses are all circumstantial in reference to ἀπεστερήμεθα and the succeeding clauses. δέ is omitted by Dindorf, Franke, and Whiston. — 28. 24. χώρας οἰκείας, *territory that belongs to us.* The Scholiast refers it particularly to Amphipolis. It may also include other places of which Philip had robbed the Athenians. — 26. οὓς...οὗτοι, *and allies whom we had gained in the war, these men* (the above-mentioned worthies) *have lost in time of peace,* that is, when war was not openly declared. For the transfer of συμμάχους from the antecedent to the relative clause, see C. 553 ; G. 154 ; H. 809. — P. 31, l. 1. τηλικοῦτον ἠσκήκαμεν. Cf. I. 9 : ηὐξήσαμεν ἡμεῖς καὶ κατεστήσαμεν τηλικοῦτον. See also II. 4. — 29. 2. ἀλλ' ὦ τᾶν. A remark interposed by an imagined respondent. This is not infrequent in Demosthenes. So Cicero often introduces by *ast* an objection which he would anticipate and forestall. — 5. τὰς ἐπάλξεις, *the parapets which we are plastering, and the roads which we are repairing, and fountains, and fooleries.* λήρους is thus used elsewhere also by Demosthenes to throw contempt on a series of things previously enumerated. Plato uses φλυαρίας in the same way. The omission of the article with κρήνας and λήρους intensifies the contempt. Sauppe charges the orator with injustice. The supply of a country so arid as Attica with water was no trifling matter, and yet it was the merest trifle relatively to the rights and liberties of the people. — 7. ἀποβλέψατε, *turn your eyes.* — τοὺς...πολιτευομένους. *Those who direct their statesmanship to these objects.* Eubulus and his associates seem to have valued themselves on such improvements. — 8. οἱ μέν, e. g. Demades, Æschines, Phryno, and Philocrates. — 9. οἱ δέ. Demades rose from the rank of a sailor, Æschines was an inferior actor, etc. — ἔνιοι. In the oration against Meidias, Demosthenes says that he (Meidias) has built a house at Eleusis of such magnitude as to overshadow all others in the place.

30. 13. τί δή ποτε, *why in the world then.* δή referring the question directly to what precedes, and ποτέ emphasizing it. Al. δήποτε, and δή ποθ'. — **14.** τὸ μὲν πρῶτον, *formerly indeed*, strictly, *at the first.* Al. πρότερον. — τολμῶν, *inasmuch as they dared.* It is the implied reason why they were masters of the politicians, etc. — καὶ στρατεύεσθαι, *to serve in the army also*, as well as to discharge their civil duties. — αὐτός, *in person.* — **16.** κύριος αὐτός, *were themselves the disposers of all the emoluments.* — **17.** ἀγαπητὸν...ἑκάστῳ, *and each of the others* (of the leading public men) *was well satisfied.* ἑκάστῳ is dative of the doer after ἀγαπητὸν ἦν. — **31. 21.** ἐκνενευρισμένοι is understood by some as referring to material resources, which are the *nerves* and sinews of war, and so explained by the words which follow. But besides being somewhat tautological, that would leave out the main point. Better understood of the character of the Athenians, and opposed to στρατεύεσθαι τολμῶν αὐτός = *enervated.* — **23.** ἐν ὑπηρέτου.. γεγένησθε, *have sunk into the position of an underling and a hanger-on.* Cf. II. 14, and note there. — ἀγαπῶντες is antithetic to ἀγαπητόν above : not, like their ancestors, well satisfied with some share in the public honors and offices, but *delighted if these men* (Eubulus and company) *allow you to participate in the theoric money or exhibit the Boëdromia.* πέμψωσιν is here used in a pregnant sense, viz. to celebrate with processions and parade ; hence our word *pomp.* The aorist denotes a special celebration (probably with unusual pomp by Eubulus the previous year) : the present in μεταδιδῶσι denotes a customary action. The Boëdromia was a festival in honor of Apollo Boëdromius on the seventh day of the month Boëdromion (answering to latter half of September and first half of October, and named from this festival). For further particulars see Dic. Antiq. Whiston reads βοΐδια. — **25.** ἀνδρειότατον, *manliest of all.* It is, of course, ironical. Al. ἀνανδρότατον. — **26.** προσοφείλετε, *you feel under obligations to them too.* προς- = *besides, too.* — **27.** καθείρξαντες, *having cooped you up in the city itself*, as in a cage. — P. 32, l. 1. τιθασεύουσι, *keep you tame, making you submissive to themselves.* — χειροήθεις = mansuetos. There is a manifest allusion throughout to wild beasts and their masters. — **32.** ἔστι δ' οὐδέποτ', *but it is never possible, I think, to form a great and noble spirit while engaged in small and mean pursuits ; for of what sort soever the occupations of men may be, such also must of necessity their spirit be.* The application of this great ethical maxim is to the

Athenians, who lived a life of pleasure and amusement. — 5. **ταῦτα** is the object of **εἰπόντι** and of **πεποιηκότων**. It is placed at the beginning for emphasis, and without a connective (asyndeton) as an illustration of the foregoing maxim : *these things, for instance — verily I should not be surprised if greater harm should come to me for having mentioned them than to those who have caused their existence.* — **τῶν πεποιηκότων** = ἢ τοῖς πεποιηκόσι. Cf. C. 511, b ; H. 586, b.

33. 10. **Ἐὰν...ἔτι.** An abbreviation for ἐὰν οὖν, εἰ καὶ μὴ πρότερον ἠθελήσατε, ἀλλὰ νῦν γ᾽ ἔτι. *If then, though you would not before, yet now after all you will.* So Phil. I. 9. Whiston. — 13. **ἀφορμαῖς ἐπί** = *as means to obtain.* — **ἴσως ἄν, ἴσως.** Cf. note, I. 19. — 16. **λημμάτων**, *receipts*, here in contempt = *such paltry receipts as these*, described above, § 31. Cf. II. 28, and note there. — **ἃ...ἔοικε**, *which resemble delicate morsels given by physicians to the sick.* — **σιτίοις** may be regarded as a diminutive of σῖτος, and so rendered as above ; it is rendered *delicacies* by Whiston ; *diet* by Kennedy and Heslop ; *gruel* by Champlin. — **ἀσθενοῦσιν** is erased or bracketed by several editors as standing between τοῖς and the emphatic word (σιτίοις), to which it should belong. — 17. **καὶ γὰρ...καὶ** = *for as...so.* — 18. **ἐκεῖνα**, sc. σίτια ; ταῦτα, sc. these pittances from the theoric fund. — **ταῦτα...νέμεσθε** may be rendered, *these allowances*, with Heslop. — 20. **οὔτ᾽...ἐᾷ**, *nor permit you to renounce them, and do something else.* — 34. 22. **οὐκοῦν...λέγεις**, *well, then, you propose pay, do you not ?* sc. for military service, instead of the allowances which the orator has just been satirizing. It is substantially the same question which he supposes some one to ask in I. 19 : σὺ γράφεις ταῦτ᾽ εἶναι στρατιωτικά ; but he answers the question more boldly here : *yes, and I also propose that there be immediately the same arrangement for all* the citizens, to wit, that you all do your duty, and then all receive the public money as freely as you now do, but receive it as pay for service. Thus the orator avoids any suggestion of *taking away* their receipts from the treasury. It was customary to pay citizen soldiers as well as mercenaries. — 24. **τὴν αὐτὴν σύνταξιν**, cf. I. 20 : μίαν σύνταξιν τὴν αὐτὴν τοῦ τε λαμβάνειν καὶ τοῦ ποιεῖν τὰ δέοντα ; but then, in the first Oration, he only says it *ought* to be so, while here he directly proposes it. — 25. **τὸ μέρος**, *his share.* — **τοῦθ᾽** is predicate after **ὑπάρχοι**, *may be that, whatever it be, which the state may require.* Al. παρέχοι. — **ἔξεστιν, κ. τ. λ.**, *if we are allowed to be at peace, remaining at home better, because released from the necessity of doing*

*anything dishonorable by reason of want: if some such emergency as
the present* (the war of Olynthus) *arise, serving in person as a soldier
from the same receipts* (from the theoric fund), *as it is his duty to do
in the service of his country: if one of us* (al. ὑμῶν, you) *is beyond the
age for doing military duty, what such an one now receives irregularly
without being of any service, still receiving in a just regulation for
overseeing and administering what requires to be done.* This is the
outline of the orator's proposed system in its adaptation to the neces-
sities of the state and the circumstances of the individual citizen in
these supposed cases. The supposition, in each case, however, is
briefly hinted instead of being expressed in a conditional form; and
the conclusion in each case, instead of being in the *form* of an apodosis,
is appended in a participial clause. See a similar construction in § 18;
also in the familiar and famous passage of De Corona, § 198: πράττεταί
τι τῶν ὑμῖν δοκούντων συμφέρειν· ἄφωνος Αἰσχίνης, κ. τ. λ. Our orator
is fond of sentences so constructed. The participles all agree with
ἕκαστος, and, as appositives of τοῦθ', constitute the predicates after
ὑπάρχοι. As the participial clauses distribute τοῦθ', so the clauses
which imply the conditions may be regarded as distributing ὅτου
δέοιτο ἡ πόλις. These last clauses are made interrogative in some,
though not the most nor the best editions. Some MSS. have λαμ-
βανέτω, but S and some others have λαμβάνων, which is followed by
Dindorf, Whiston, Franke, Sauppe, Westermann, and Rehdantz. —
35. 7. ὅλως δέ, κ. τ. λ., *and in fine* (in general) *without taking from
or adding to* (existing laws), *only removing a little the irregularity*
(that exists) *I have brought* (by the arrangement above proposed) *the
state into order by making one and the same order for receiving money,*
etc. — **12. οὐκ ἔστιν ὅπου...εἶπον,** *I have nowhere said* (in any part
of this oration) *that we ought to distribute to those who are doing nothing what belongs to those who will do, nor that we ought ourselves to be
idle, unemployed and penniless and only to* HEAR *that the mercenaries of such an one are victorious,* and thus, provided the report is
true, doing the service and reaping the rewards which belong rather
to you. — **τοῦ δεῖνος.** Cf. ὁ δεῖνα, Ol. II. 31, and note there. The
orator is here supposed to allude to Charidemus, who was at this
time in command at Olynthus. — **36. 17. τὸν ποιοῦντα...ὑπὲρ ὑμῶν,**
e. g. the mercenary soldier. — **19. μὴ παραχωρεῖν,** *not to withdraw
from the post* (or role) *of virtue which your ancestors bequeathed to
you.* For the position of τῆς ἀρετῆς (in the relative clause) see C.

551, c; G. 154; H. 809. — 23. σχεδὸν = fere. Cf. Cic. de Nat.
De. 1, 16: exposui fere. —ἔλοισθε. This oration, like the First Ol.,
closes with a prayer. See note ibid. The attentive and appreciative
reader cannot withhold his approval from the critical judgment of
Grote, who, after giving a copious analysis, which fills several pages,
laments that his space confines him to this brief and meagre ab-
stract, and pronounces "the third Olynthiac of Demosthenes one of
the most splendid harangues ever delivered."